in search of the pleasure palace

also by marc almond

tainted life

marc almond

in search of the pleasure palace

disreputable travels

pan books

First published 2004 by Sidgwick & Jackson

This edition published 2013 by Pan Books
an imprint of Pan Macmillan, a division of Macmillan Publishers Limited
Pan Macmillan, 20 New Wharf Road, London N1 9RR
Basingstoke and Oxford
Associated companies throughout the world
www.panmacmillan.com

ISBN 978-1-4472-4916-0

A CIP catalogue record for this book is available from
the British Library.

Typeset by SetSystems Ltd, Saffron Walden, Essex

Printed and bound by CPI Group (UK) Ltd, Croydon, CR0 4YY

All Pan Macmillan titles are available from
www.panmacmillan.com
or from Bookpost by telephoning +44 (0)1624 677237

My thanks go to the following people: ML for his patience and good humour; Scott Ewalt for his New York guidance (he just told me the venues ShowWorld and Stella's have finally been closed down since writing about them in this book – is there anywhere left?); Misha Kucherenko for the Russian album and for his guidance and friendship; Sergey Ignatov for being a special friend and for doing so much for me while I was staying in Moscow. To all my Russian friends too numerous to name, but especially to Natasha for finding me an apartment; to Sergei Afrika in St Petersburg and Dima Tolkanov; Pierre et Gilles for the cover, and for being an inspiration always. To Beto in Mexico City and all my friends there. To Vicki Wickham, of course, who might get round to calling me, and to Nita @ POW. To everyone in LA, especially Chi Chi. To Anita Sarko and Darren Walsh in New York. To so many London friends and associates – Nick Timms, Gordon Wise (even though you deserted me), Natalie Jerome (for picking up the pieces), Pan Macmillan for letting me write this book, Neal Whitmore, Jamie McLoud, Roland Mouret (style enforcer) and to BisXIII Records and Mehdi for their continued support. A special thanks to Kate and Michelle for the website www.marcalmond.co.uk. And finally, of course, thanks to all my fans who have supported me throughout.

Permissions Acknowledgements

Burt Bacharach/Hal David 'I'll never fall in love again' reproduced with kind permission of Universal MCA Ltd/Windswept

'Just a Gigolo', words by Julius Brammer (English translation by Irving Caesar) and music by Leonello Casucci © 1930, Wiener Boheme Verlag/ de Sylva Brown and Henderson Inc, Germany/Irving Caesar Music Corp. Reproduced by permission of EMI music publishing, London WC2H OQY. (25%) Warner Chappell Music Ltd, London W6 8BS. Reproduced by permission of International Music Publications Ltd. All rights reserved.

Contents

Prologue

'Reality is not what we see, but what we discover,
or in my case rediscover'

•

Since writing this book many of the places, locations and
names may have changed or gone for good in the name of
change. It is in part a guide to all those places around the
world that have meant something to me: it is also a journal
of my life over the last four years. If I'm being honest there
were times when I never knew what it was about, or what I
was trying to achieve with it; all I knew was that I wanted
to share some of my thoughts, experiences and insights in
some vague hope they might hold a common thread, or at
least let you, the reader, escape for a while. It is also of
course about navigating a way through my midlife crisis but
that will become apparent to you. My publisher wanted me
to use this prologue to define what the book was about, but
I was reluctant to do that. It's just about places I've been to,
people I've met, experiences undertaken, opinions I've
formed and the surreality that life has thrown up at me – a
personal journal made up of snapshots of my life.

I like to think of it as a box of chocolates left on the
coffee table – occasionally you may delight in finding a
strawberry fondue, a caramel cream or a cherry liqueur . . .
but you might want to leave the praline or nougat.

At the end, should you reach it, perhaps you'll venture to some of the places I've been to and have your own experiences.

That's the best I could hope for.

Marc Almond

1

Too Old to Die Young

Was that it?

What am I talking about? A defining moment in life. In midlife.

It was as if I had just seen my life flicker past brightly, like a film on a screen, all hope and passion and achievement condensed and illuminated for a second – and before I could cry out 'There was a happy day, a bad one, a regret, a smile' the film had melted and burned.

From the outer edge of life you look back and think, was that it?

And a silence begins to weave a strange sound in and out, in a great vast loom, crossing, recrossing, making a final pattern of emptiness.

One day it all becomes painfully clear that you're middle-aged, and that instant becomes a defining moment in your life.

And though I kept telling myself, over and over, I'm only just in my forties, I couldn't find anything positive in the words.

What the hell am I going to do from now on?

I imagined myself sitting and reminiscing about who I used to be in my glory days, the maudlin ranting of a former pop star in the late Indian summer of his career. It was all too short and not that sweet.

Still making records, trying to reach out to the fickle

public whose appetites have grown ever more ravenous as they pick at your bones and spit you out, suck you dry and then throw you away like a soggy old condom down the S-bend of life, only (if you're lucky, they say) you end up in the TV sewer of cable, guesting on the next reality show or worse still on *Never Mind the Buzzcocks*, sitting in that identity parade to be singled out for humiliation.

Not me, no thank you.

But if not these things then what happens to a former pop star like me. 'Pop star'?

I gave that moniker up years ago. Artist sounds better.

What happens to an artist like me – the king of sleazy listening?

•

I just don't know, other than to take the time to re-evaluate my life.

If I'm honest I must say that I am approaching middle age with fear and dread. Now before you stop me and say, 'Well, aren't you in the thick of middle age already?' I would like to remind you that 40 is the new 30 or even younger if you're wearing well. And middle age is now around 50 because, as everyone knows, life expectancy is 102 or thereabout.

What I guess (read as 'know deep down') is that I'm having a midlife crisis, and I know the exact moment it began.

The day started as these days do, quite like any other.

It was a crisp February morning in 2001 and I was in the midst of promoting a single I had out, doing those endless rounds of interviews and appearances to let people know I was not only still alive but making records too.

Despite my reservations I was due to appear on a daytime TV show that shall remain nameless. I was booked for an interview and performance of the said song.

The car collected me late morning and took me to the

studio. As I sat in the dressing room, desperately applying more and more make-up, waiting for rehearsal, there came a knock on the door. The hostess popped her head in, said thanks for doing the show and, noticing my nervousness, reassured me that it would be great, it was a terrific audience.

The floor manager collected me and took me on set, which is a gaudy recreation of a cross-section of the presenter's own home, complete with sitting room, kitchen and conservatory, garishly decorated in colours that B&Q would label 'ripe peach', 'lemon summer' and 'meringue beige'. Then all too quickly I'm sitting on the fuchsia sofa discussing my sordid past in muted tones, all leading to a mumsy crescendo of a performance of my single in the kitchen just stage left of the tumble-dryer.

It was then it happened.

Like a car accident – too quickly, you can't stop it, you can't do anything. Mouthing the words and half watching myself on the monitor, I quite simply felt I was losing control. All I could do was wait for the ride to end, the song to finish. What was I doing? It all seemed so pointless and futile – the grand scheme of things, life, the universe, meaning, purpose, it all seemed utterly insignificant.

And there is was. The onset of my midlife crisis. And it also marked the onset of a reoccurring, horrible dream.

I am standing in front of a mirror and staring back at me is my face but slowly it transforms into someone else, yet somehow remains recognizably me. I study the mirror and I'm becoming Ken Barlow, the character from *Coronation Street*. And instead of a leather jacket I'm wearing a woolly cardigan which I pull tighter around myself. It feels comfortable, cosy, staid, and it fits perfectly.

The first time the dream ended I interpreted it as a sign that I had become old, and life had not only caught up with me but had overtaken me in the fast lane. And it's roaring ahead.

I see so much irony and weirdness in
the world that I just can't shut up.
I can't not say anything.

Looking back I blame all the drugs I took. I gave them
up a few years ago and went through what people call rehab,
which I prefer to call, bluntly, incarceration in a mental
institution. The rehabilitation process took the thrill of the
drugs away. Now they don't hold the same attraction,
replaced by guilt or something akin to it. Like a lover that
you've had intimacy with too many times, there's nowhere
left to go. The love's gone flat.

The problem is that drugs took up all the time (acquiring
them, using them, recovering from them) you now find you
have free to dwell on your life and all the problems it throws
up. And all the memories of being on drugs have been
eroded by the drugs themselves, creating a hole in your past.
And then suddenly you're middle-aged, wondering what
happened to your life, facing a crisis of identity and place in
the world and what it's all about.

Time, energy, age. I look enviously (just sometimes) at
my younger friends, who have energy to waste. Not that I
actually want to be in my twenties again; I would just like
to feel that time wasn't running away on me. It's great in
one way to surround yourself with younger friends, hoping
some youth dust rubs off. But come Saturday night when
they call to go clubbing and Cilla's just introducing the
couple from hell on *Blind Date*, something's gotta give and
these days it's not Cilla. I make my excuses and look in the
mirror, pulling the proverbial cardigan tighter and slipping
into my carpet slippers.

I suspect that I know what I'm feeling has to do with
suddenly finding myself trapped in midlife: the door to a
sunny bright day locked, the only one open leading to old

age. I reluctantly try the handle, push the door slightly open and peek in – posters adorn the wall advertising subscriptions to *Saga* magazine, cruises around the fjords, walk-in baths and the merits of denture adhesive.

Suddenly Dora Bryan waves, and Thora Hird beckons from a Stannah stairlift.

I pull the door closed and panic sets in.

•

A midlife crisis for anyone is bad enough but for a 'known' person, even if it may not actually be more difficult, it carries additional baggage. Let me explain.

There is the public face of Marc Almond. There are still fans out there who consider me an icon and sex symbol (yes, I know it might strike some of you as strange, but I assure you it is true), and this adds additional pressure. You see, you create an image and then you find that you are trapped in it. If part of you finds it appealing, that only compounds the problem.

When you dance with the Devil, the Devil doesn't change – he only changes you. Soon you become the person who you want people to believe you are.

And then you believe you are.

And the illusion you create takes over, and the edges in your mind blur. The photos become more retouched in an attempt to recreate what you once were. And once more I find myself struggling to resist the call of the early eighties. For some pop whores grown portly on the rewards of yesterday's fame and apathy, squeezing into yesterday's leather leggings is not usually a good idea, but it's the only choice. Nor is it a good idea to create a heyday hairstyle, especially mine.

So the more I thought about it, the less I knew how to overcome my crisis.

I had to make a decision. Were the options really only to carry on recording albums that fewer and fewer people would care about, to accept this emptiness inside me as just part of me that I had to live with (like Anne Boleyn's sixth digit), to waste money on psychologists who would provide only cryptic answers; grow old disgracefully, dutifully taking my place on *Never Mind The Buzzcocks* and the eighties revival tours?

Or?

Or was there a way of moving on by going back in a different kind of way?

And that was how this journey began.

All those places I had visited that had inspired me; perhaps they could inspire anew. Perhaps by revisiting such places I might find something I sensed I'd lost, left behind. And by writing about my journey I might find a way to navigate through my midlife crisis, maybe even help others too – I felt uplifted and inspired. And at worst it would be a chance to run away. But no, this was actually a matter of rising to the challenge. It was time to give something back to anyone who felt like I did.

If at the end of the journey I still felt the same, I would accept the inevitable and get out my chicken-bone necklace and bangles, crimp what's left of my hair and do what needed to be done.

But in the meantime, before I set out on my travels around the world on my inward journey, I had to do something that I had never dared to before. It was now or never. I picked up the phone and made an appointment with the cosmetic surgeon.

'Reinvent me in my own image.'

•

As I lay on the operating table Dr Karuthers slipped the syringe into my arm and asked me to count backwards from ten.

Ten.

Nine

Eiiiigggght . . .

•

Life is punctuated with turning points.

Your first word.

Your first step.

Your first kiss.

Isn't it strange that more often than not you can't remember them?

But your first cosmetic surgery operation . . .

•

'Wake up, Mr Almond.'

I opened my eyes slowly.

'It's over. It went very well. The nurse will take you to your room and I'll come and see you later.'

The ceiling flowed over me as the trolley moved down the corridor.

I don't know how long I slept, but when I woke I felt like I was drowning in a sea of blood and snot and that my throat had been torn out. I vomited black congealed blood. A plaster cast covered my nose and face, forcing the swollen tissue to take to the mould underneath. I struggled out of bed to look in the bathroom mirror. I gasped in disbelief at my reflection.

Then I thought of all those frail rich old women who haunt the food hall at Harrods, how they must have coped with one painful surgical procedure after another. The clinic brochure had described the after-effect of surgery as 'mildly uncomfortable, with occasional soreness'.

No reference had been made to the reality, which was horrifying.

A week later I was back in the hospital to have the mask and bandages removed. I had stayed hidden in the house for the whole week, sustained on a diet of trepidation, self-pity and banal daytime television. The nurse removed my bandages, repeatedly explaining that I must not be upset or surprised by my appearance as the swelling had not gone down. The surgeon, apparently never attending an unveiling – wisely, as I can imagine people's immediate reaction if mine was anything to go by – had sent his kind regards.

Then she reached for the mirror and held it up to my face.

Oh God, what had I done?

Two images came into my head.

The first was a scene from Brian De Palma's film *Carrie* when Carrie's mother warns her against going to the prom night with the fatalistic words, 'They're all gonna laugh at you, they're all gonna laugh at you.'

The second was again a scene from a film but this time from Scorcese's *Raging Bull*, a point where the character Jake La Motta has lost his boxing crown and his face is a mass of swelling and bruising.

But too late now. Maybe after the swelling had gone down I would feel different. Hell, it just looked worse than it really was, that had to be it.

The journey was already beginning, and I had tentatively taken the first step.

2

First Steps

'And I'll stay off Verlaine too;
he was always chasing Rimbauds'

•

After a couple more weeks hidden in the house, the swelling subsided and the bruising faded. My new nose took shape, and I liked it. It was sort of the same but different. In fact the real indication came when I ventured out. People never noticed the change but commented on how good I was looking. I paraded my new nose around town and the general response was positive. I felt at last I could get on with my life without my nose getting in the way of my face.

It was time to move on and get started. Time to find out what part of my past could enthuse me, make me realize that life still held some thrill or purpose. Of course if this ends up being more of a trawl than a search, then so be it!

Sitting in my bedroom contemplating where to begin, pen in hand and blank page in front of me, the bedroom itself seemed as suitable a place as any.

That inner sanctum and the centre of the world. A tiny satellite around which our lives orbit.

And in the centre an island, a rock where we spend most of our lives: a bed. Where we are born, sleep, fall sick, make love, dream.

The womb, the tomb, born and borne into.

The bed, where ideas are nurtured, events reflected upon, a place to meditate, confront fears and loss, and finally, for the lucky few, a place to die. Well, that's how I plan to go – in my bed, surrounded by the things that made me feel secure, one or two loved ones whispering tearfully.

But of course things don't always go as planned. A great example I recall is that of an all but forgotten movie star, who meticulously planned her own death: suicide naturally, desiring to be discovered laid on her glamorous bed surrounded by white lilies, a timeless still from some undiscovered movie, her life ebbing away from the barbiturate overdose. Unfortunately the best laid plans and so forth . . . there she lay, waiting to slip into legend, when she felt the urge to vomit, lurched towards the bathroom, missed the bowl and spewed across the tiled floor, slipping and hitting her head on the cistern and collapsed, her head trapped between the toilet and the wall.

The perfect meeting of glamour and squalor. Her career and her death relegated to B-movie status.

Elvis Presley too died on the lavatory, a heart attack while straining to expel a hard clay-like faeces from his blocked colon. It must have been a mammoth task made all the more difficult by the years of fried banana and peanut butter sandwiches, loyally served to him by his black maid, like some unsuspecting host bird driven to exhaustively feeding a cuckoo into obesity. I know this is likely to be true because after visiting Graceland and sampling one of these gourmet delectations I too was severely constipated for several days.

No, a far preferable way to end my days would be like that of Marlene Dietrich, ensconced in bed for the final decade of her life, surrounded by everything she needed – bedpans, stocked fridges within reach, and a telephone to the outside world from which she could conduct the business of preserving her legend. She would phone all manner of people, regardless of the time or inconvenience to them, inconsiderately dishing out words of Teutonic wisdom. A fabulous monster.

That's how I want to end it.

So it is, that the beginning of my journey and, God willing, the end, will both be in my bedroom.

Stars shimmer as they grow dimmer.

There's a television in my bedroom, a window to an astonishing array of stimulation and enlightenment – or so I thought.

Aim the remote.

Be it late night television, or early morning, depending on where you look you'll be able to find a veritable array of the same things.

Docusoaps. Sex files. G-string divas. Strippers. Carnal delights.

Lowlifes, hookers, transvestites, now so familiar across an array of channels, role models for a desensitized generation.

I thought at first it might, if not offer me the answers I was looking for, at least afford some stimulation or inspiration, and even distraction.

It doesn't take a genius to work out that television won't offer any answers to my midlife crisis, but it might point me in the direction I need to go. But television is the great lie, and nowhere is it more apparent than when dealing with sex, the single greatest marketing tool known to advertising executives and rating moguls.

Take sex on television – there is none.

It pretends to stimulate but doesn't dare, unlike, say, pornographic movies whose sole aim is to stimulate: television stimulation is like a porn movie but with the porn taken out. It is just about wasted time.

Television will do anything to mislead you about all things sexual, usually in the guise of information, docusoap, health. Even daytime TV is in on the ploy with features on panties, bras or underpants modelled by well-proportioned people. Features on breast or testicular cancer are often little more than an excuse to show naked flesh, the host even fondling the man's balls in the name of medical information. Sure they'll blind you with their health concerns and the need to stop blushing, titter, titter, I saw a nipple, oops!

Worse still is slot after slot filled with people revealing their secret desires, which almost always involve them wanting to be lap dancers or strippers, always ready at the drop of a hat to peel off down to market-stall leopard-skin thong while a shell-suited audience whoop and holler and attempt to coordinate their hands in a clapping motion.

Then I did something that never occurred to me before. I turned the TV off. Suddenly the room was eerily silent and still.

Disillusioned with TV I decided to search the Internet for guidance. I typed into the search engine 'Midlife Crisis' and found myself with the following choices: Viagra, Ejaculation Delay Creams, Hair Dye for Grey, Insolvency Brokers, Herbal Remedies, and 'How You Can Quickly and Easily Discover If Your Mate Is Cheating On You' . . .

'When I had journeyed half of our life's way, I found myself within a shadowed forest, for I had lost the path that does not stray' – Dante.

All the while pop-ups kept appearing offering sex, all manner of sex aids, breast enlargements and congratulations on 'Having won today's prize with sixty seconds to claim', and sex again.

Sex on the web. Of all the joyless experiences thrown up this has to be up there with the worst of them. It is hard to imagine what kind of generation will emerge from the

Internet years – I was considered in my youth as a bad influence on a generation and all I had access to was a copy of *Health & Efficiency* magazine and watching *Les Enfants du Paradis*. So be warned.

Now you can log on and within minutes be transported to a squalid room in Manila where an Asian prostitute splays her legs, fingers herself on your command, the image sputtering into focus as she speaks to you in a cold techno voice.

Or you can look at all manner of filth and depravation. I have for the purpose of this book seen sites showing men with men, men with women, women with women, women with dogs or horses (there seem to be no pornographic images of men with mares or bitches), people masturbating in their own excrement, penises nailed to headboards, black-boards, ironing boards, breasts clamped down with clothes pegs, gran bangs and even pregnant women breast-feeding grown men.

I ask you.

For a while it fills a curiosity but then even that goes. The net for me is quite an unsexy experience. Being dyslexic, typing and masturbating present all kinds of problems and besides, I fear tapping the wrong key and finding myself on one of those sites that set off alarm bells in Scotland Yard, and have the police knocking on your door at six in the morning with bin bags and technicians ready to investigate your hard-drive.

The Internet, like the TV, is just a trick of the light.

What seems to have happened to sex is that it's lost its sexiness. We have become desexualized. Spayed. Explicit has replaced erotic.

3

Calm Down!

There is an expression in boxing:
'Bury me with a puncher'

•

I view the current climate of this country with a mixture of bemusement and despair. Britain has always been cynical, but now the cynicism is like a shifting malaise affecting everyone, and even I find myself falling with the sickness. Ours is a country defined by celebrity and scandal, a culture of superficiality and meanness, of mediocrity and cruelty – perhaps to a degree it always was but now, being older and experienced, I see it more clearly. And the more I see it the less I want to do with it.

Belittlement, derision and humiliation – the catchwords of the day. Our media is the new Roman arena, where the soul is laid bare, where dashed hopes, tears and contrition are played out to a baying crowd shouting their disapproval or support, slumped on sofas pigging out on fast food, exercising our thumbs on the remote.

Careers are made or ruined this way by the public's insatiable demand for controversy or instant gratification. The serious and the seriously superficial sit side by side. Hopes and dreams and drugs and scandal vie for a headline. Allegations, rumours and speculations put yesterday's hopefuls at the mercy of tomorrow's byline. People are tried and convicted by the mob or the media, demeaned because . . . well, it's their turn.

My anger hasn't mellowed over the years. I find myself getting angry on everyone's behalf, angry and opinionated. Every dog has its day, and it's mangy dog eat mangy dog. Sometimes I feel I have the burden of the world on my shoulders, but like everyone else feel helpless to resist the current of hypocrisy washing over me. I know that times have changed: I know it's not just me. The future isn't good or bad, it's simply mediocre – an observation that resonates through me as a middle-aged man. I want to shout out, you don't have to accept this bland diet! I want to shake people and tell them there is more to life than what you're given, force-fed. But my voice goes unheard, and then people tell me to relax, that it's my age, 'Calm down, dear,' says the voice of Michael Winner. 'It's only an . . .' But I still need to get it out of my system, need someone to listen.

Travelling around the world I see the same high streets everywhere. Uniformity, corporate brand names emblazoned on every aspect of life. Every builder's crack is emblazoned with the logo CK. The irony is that the more choice we have, the less we actually have. Several coffee chains on every high street selling bascially the same coffee, more often than not two of the same type even facing each other – Starbucks opposite Starbucks, so you can choose the one in the sun-shine. The same few record shops racking up the top twenty, often without space for so-called 'alternative artists' – those that get critical acclaim but sell only a few records. I suppose I'm an alternative artist.

The music scene seems shaped by the same forces as the global high street: as well as the same clothing outlets, chemists, restaurant chains, beauty shops, Pop idol/stars are syndicated worldwide, snack-munchers pressing a red button on the remote for some interaction. Once these wannabes entertained the local pub come Saturday night; now the pub is the TV and, backed up by a team of stylists, producers, choreographers and big band orchestras, we've now got mega-big budget karaoke. The girls aspire to become Britney or Beyoncé, the boys Ronan or Robbie, performing overrehearsed standards with all the life squeezed out, like dried-up lemons, heavy on rind and pips. The songs they perform are those owned by the publishing company who liaises with the record company financing the whole debacle, and the artist ends up managed by the management company that's in bed with the record company. It's a chain of nepotism.

What bothers me is not so much the winners – there has always been manufactured pop, ever since Larry Parnes groomed his young boys in the fifties – but now we have to put up with the losers too. To put up with the wailing tears, fake emotions and the cloying pleas of 'vote for me [to show you love me]'. So much effort and energy expended for such little effect, I ask you.

Where have all the stars gone? To me a star is someone who has something extra, and something missing at the same time – flawed and extinguishable, but never mediocre. Now before you think I'm a bitter old git envious and griping at the success of this new breed of pop star, then you might be right. I just can't accept that feeling nothing is any kind of feeling. I find *Pop Idol* represents everything that saddens me about the times we live in, just as much as any other branded consumer product. It is all part of the language of advertising, which embraces the demise of privacy and sells itself as our right to know and their duty to do anything it takes or their duty to confess. Whether it is the performer breaking down and crying at failure, or a tabloid muckraking, we have come to expect all the lurid details, whether emotional or destructive. What happened to dignity? That is why I can't be a good celebrity – my dignity is important.

There were times when I opened my life and home up for scrutiny, albeit briefly, and regretted it deeply. Celebrity is not all I am. I also have a life outside of it, where I can retreat. I say 'no' to celebrity shows where you sit on a panel as a stooge and have to act like a twat. I'm a singer, that's what I do – if I can't sing on a show I won't do it. I never do celebrity! magazines that come into your home and probe down the toilet, invade your bedroom and examine your closet – it seems to me you're saying 'hello, serial killer, come on in!' Mind you, never say never because you never know.

And premieres, what are they about? The usual Cack-list suspects are trotted out from the same agencies, to slobber and grin for the camera and gush about the latest trite blockbuster or pitiful Brit film offering. I would be tempted to say it as it is – that film was crud. See, I would spoil the lie and be a 'bad celebrity' – that's just not how it's done. Or to be seen out at celebrity haunts and private clubs, arguing the merits of China White over Attica or Rouge, or some other God-awful place? Look, life is too short. Nor could I ever negotiate my admission with those immortal words, 'Don't you know who I am? I'm on the guest list', while some oh-so-imperious door whore checks her clipboard and answers 'no' to both questions.

If I do go to a club I prefer to queue and pay. I like to blend in and occasionally I convince myself that I do. But it is hard to avoid playing the celebrity game when you have a record to promote – then you just do what you have to do. I learned very early on that if you don't court the media, you find yourself left alone. But interviews still fill me with dread, especially the tabloids; it's not that I don't read them, I just don't want to be reading about myself in them.

In other words, it is easy to have privacy as a celebrity if you really want it. All you do is sidestep the circuit and have a life. I make my music and like people to accept it for what it is, and if you believe in yourself as an artist what more can you hope for? Well, perhaps a few more sales, but that's up to the public. I always expect the worst so when great things happen it is a bonus. I remain a pessimistic optimist. After twenty-five years making music and writing I feel privileged. I accept that I probably don't have a place on this world of Monoculture, but I can live with that – somehow it makes me feel more unique and relevant.

Back in the early eighties when I had that first hit record I was full of fire, aspirations and anger. I was full of ideas and excited by it all. But over two decades that optimism has been chipped away, and I have become apprehensive of the future. What has happened to us? And to me? The spirit of revolt seems to have gone astray. We're all texting each other but saying nothing – lobotomized sheep farmed by the corporations, bleating, lifetime consumers shorn of our money, kept fat on a diet of mediocrity and distracted by any noisy, colourful, empty promise.

4

Home

When I was a young naive lad of eighteen with greasy skin, a feather cut and a head full of aspirations, the one thing I knew for certain was that I could never satisfy my 'strange desires' in Southport. Not unless I frequented certain areas. Those places where unspoken goings-on were, well, going on, like the disused toilets by Hesketh Park, all but hidden from view by overhanging tree foliage, or the toilets round the back of the market near Chapel Street.

The obvious danger aside, however, toilets were never my scene. The furtive glances, the nod, the grottiness and stench of stale urine are for some people thrilling, but cottaging was not for me. (The American term for cottaging is 'a trip to the tea room', which oddly sounds more English, more genteel, in a raised-pinky-old-queerie sounding way.) But for many gay men it was virtually all there was in Southport unless, that is, you moved in the art and theatre circles.

For me, I wanted something more. I dreamed of a place where 'anything goes', a place clouded in blue smoke and bright lights, a place called London. How far away and unreachable it seemed then: like Narnia in the C. S. Lewis books. As a child I loved those stories and often climbed into my grandmother's enormous mahogany wardrobe, fighting my way through the mothballed furs to find the hidden door that would take me away. I spent so long in that closet that I never really found a way out of it and the years slid past.

As adolescence took hold so did Southport, threatening to engulf my life – I knew the longer I stayed the harder it would be to leave, and then one day more of your life is behind you than in front and then it's too late. But something told me that London was for me; small towns are for families, bringing up children, community: not for the likes of me. London was somewhere you could be all you wanted to be, could wear what you wanted without Mum ever finding out. London was filled with prostitutes, junkies, transvestites (I'd seen *The Rocky Horror Show*), freaks, and beautiful misfits. London was Sodom and Gomorrah, El Dorado, paradise and purgatory, a miasma and a phantasmagoria, a city of strange fashionable artists: oh, you get the idea – basically it was not Southport. After all, I was eighteen and trapped in a small Victorian seaside town. People from Southport could never truly be cool or beautiful, they were provincial, and since I thought myself to be above that I wanted out.

But later in life when I would deny or reinvent my past, I was to discover that a side of me would remain 'provincial' (naff): my roots always showed through. I could never be like the fashionable people in London who got it right even when it was wrong. Back then I copied the fashionable trendsetters but couldn't carry it off, certainly not in Southport. I needed to be in London where the ugly and naff aren't as naff and ugly as those in the sticks. People in London seemed so cool, sexually ambivalent, experienced; drugs might have made them look wasted but it was a look. Even the worst haircut there made a statement. I wanted to exude that certain something I saw in Londoners. Upon hearing my desires Southport locals would grimace and shudder; 'What you want to go to that bloody place?' or

'You want your head examining, nowt there but muggers and queers' – and that was exactly my point.

When people asked me, 'What you going to do in London?' I would shrug, I had no idea. What they should have been asking me was, 'When you go to London what will you be wearing?' That was my main concern. I knew Londoners could be mean; after all, the reality was my clothes either came from Clobber or Freeman's and Grattans catalogues, and maybe someone in London could get away with wearing them but I didn't have the irony. Since that first trip to London when I felt like an awkward rent boy down from up north to turn a trick, I've never been able to shake that feeling of provinciality; it clings to the bottom of my shoe and no matter what I do I still catch the occasional whiff. Inverted snobbery I suppose, because despite my fabulous art-school training, my pop success, a world of experiences and opportunities, a streetwise demeanour and a style I can call my own, there are still occasional moments when I feel awkward, out of my depth.

I'll give you an example: I might be in the company of some London-born, young, upcoming artist – you know the sort, confident, good-looking, unkempt while being painfully and effortlessly cool – who's showing me his new art piece (the sort of nonsense Brian Sewell deplores, in this case a pile of decomposing dandelion leaves inside a glass cube entitled 'Tetramorph No. 7'). And he's explaining it 'symbolizes that each journey is the consequence of unbearable longing, blah, blah, blah'; but I'm not listening because I'm thinking, how can he be so cool and hip, and why do I feel intimidated and self-conscious. Then suddenly he's looking at me expectantly.

'Well? Do you agree?' he asks.

And of course I've not been listening and fumble for words.

'Oh yes, exactly,' I say. He slips me his card, asking me if
I might be interested in acquiring the piece. So I ask how
much it is, and suddenly he looks at me disdainfully for
suggesting that he could ever put a price on his art, sighs
resignedly and moves off.

So I suddenly feel really awkward and uncool for bringing
up the price, and maybe it was a naff thing to do but I still
feel it's a fair question. As I edge my way out, I remind
myself that I may not be the coolest person around and I
might be out of my depth with the in-crowd but I know a
pile of shit when I see it.

•

Sorry, I digress. All that was ahead of me. I'm stuck in
Southport, and London seemed so out of reach; the journey
there would take three years via Leeds. When I eventually
moved to London I knew I would never leave. And it would
take me almost two decades to fully appreciate what an
incredible place it is. And maybe you have to travel widely
to eventually understand that.

Glass, concrete, shadow and light, historical and modern,
a city of so many deep dark sexy and bloody secrets. The
best city in the world.

The taxi takes me along the Embankment and across
Waterloo Bridge, one of the most breathtaking views in the
world. Later, crossing London Bridge to Southwark, I can
feel the weight of past centuries as I look down at Tower
Bridge. It reminds me that I am just a lad from Southport
who made good, in London, to live amongst its landmarks.
This then is the 'big smoke', talked about in my Southport
days with a sneer. Even then I already had my mirrors and
illusions, so I guess all I needed was the smoke. And where
there's smoke there's fire. Writing forces you to examine the

past and there you find memories you haven't recalled for over twenty years.

In my Southport Art College days there was a mysterious young man who started halfway through the first term. His name was Fred, though I suspect it may have been a nickname since he was so un-Fred like (just as my nickname was Bill). Anyway, I suspected it was a false name, as I bet he was running away from something or someone. So, we shall call him Frederick, which is just a little more royal and slightly more fey and therefore far more appropriate. Frederick was handsome, with long hair and a superior cut. This was the seventies so a comparison would be Tadzio, the elusive beautiful object of the leery old composer Ashenbach in Visconti's film *Death in Venice*. Dirk Bogarde stars as Aschenbach, a celebrated, ageing composer entranced by the ethereal beauty of a Polish youth who seems to embody his ideals of physical perfection and spiritual purity. He succumbs to a fateful obsession, basically stalking him. Of course Aschenbach would be arrested in double time these days, his photo splashed across the *News of the World*: but this was the seventies and no one dwelt on such things.

Death in Venice was an eye-opener for me as a teenager. On the surface not much happens but what Visconti has done is celebrate homosexuality as a spiritual, intellectual quest, rather than an up-the-back alley sex fest. 'It is a masterful, symphonic study of sensuality and decay, gorgeous, sumptuous and slow as an arthritic turtle.' It opened a window in the heart for those of us who wanted to discover more about ourselves, but were trapped in situations (Southport) where we had no outlet to express these feelings, let alone give them a name. I was young, dumb and full of cum and I identified with both Ashenbach and Tadzio. The older protagonist, the young man adored and pursued.

I suppose, like a young heterosexual boy who wants the tuition and adoration of an older woman (The Mrs Robinson syndrome), the same applies for some adolescent gays.

Which brings us back to Frederick, an elusive free spirit with his slight air of indignation and superiority (perhaps because he came from London). I gravitated towards Frederick, and soon discovered that he had an Aschenbach all of his own – a sponsor, a mentor, an adviser, call it what you want – who had enrolled him in Southport Art College where his artistic harbouring could be nurtured. For what other reason would he be in Southport? I suspected they had run away together to start a new life, despite the fact that his companion was extremely old (mid-thirties, which in the seventies was like being mid-sixties today). I held with this running away theory because it was fabulous and delicious and dangerous, and fuelled my adolescent romantic views that there might be some hope for me too.

Anyway, having acquainted myself with Frederick I was soon invited to his flat, a shadowy high-ceilinged ground-floor conversion in Southport. Bare floorboards, Erté lamps, framed erotic photos of Frederick, scantily clad, holding Nijinsky fawn-like poses – all so Bohemian. It seemed I was to discover that Frederick aspired to be a ballet dancer (more Isadora Duncan than Fonteyn), and once when his punter, sorry, sponsor was out he performed a dance just for me – a nude introspective piece. Again I thought of Dirk Bogarde but this time in the film *The Night Porter*, the scene where his effeminate Nazi accomplice dances impromptu while Dirk's character works the follow spot, just before he injects his bare buttock with morphine or something equally decadent.

So Frederick danced around the room like a nymph possessed, culminating in a grand jeté into the bedroom where he collapsed exhausted (read as artistically drained) on the double bed. He turned round to catch my eye, and then reached surreptitiously into the bedside drawer and invited me to peruse a selection of photographs of himself in naked poses. Provocatively, he looked up at me peering naively at his exposed reared buttocks. And I'm sorry to say I froze. I was unable to read the signs. I can't believe that I was ever that naive, that this courtship ritual, this mating prelude, failed to coax me into the sex act. Southportness showed me up and the gulf was far too wide to breach.

What a missed chance. Tears, regrets, curtain! God, when I look back, how many moments have I misread; I could quite easily chew myself up with bitterness. But knowing me, had I succumbed it would no doubt have ended up in an awkward fumble and flaccid erection, chided, prematurely ejected and rejected by the worldly Frederick and just another conquest to add to his collection. Better a love unrequited (I tell myself unconvincingly).

But when he told me he had not only lived in London, but actually in Soho, he grew ever more exotic. Soho, the centre of the world. He described where he had lived, in a neon-lit flat in Archer Street, overlooking Charlie's Casino. How much more fabulous could it get? He told me about the police raids on the prostitutes who lived downstairs. Oh my God, I thought, not only had he lived in Soho, London, in a neon-illuminated room overlooking a casino, he'd also lived alongside prostitutes, junkies, pimps and creatures of the night, characters I imagined straight out of the Jean Genet novels that David Bowie had urged me to read through his songs.

I made up my mind, there and then, that I too would live in Soho in such a room and with such lowlife neighbours. And so my goal was set. Then I would be all knowing and glowing and could look down with a superior air at people from the provinces. And do you know what? It came true.

I buried my northern twang and looked down my nose (which in those pre-op days was a long way down) and became a pretentious pain in the ass. But I suspect Frederick and I were, in the end, cut from the same cloth. I would have liked to show him my Soho flat all those years later, not overlooking a casino but Raymond's Revue Bar – top that!

Soho – once even just saying the word filled me with an illicit thrill. I was after all part of it, albeit a bit player in its rich and colourful history. Now I feel like a visitor even, on occasions, like a tourist. My heart doesn't have a place here anymore and I don't belong. Soho has moved on, and in many ways it seems so have I. Recently, it has regained or reclaimed some of its seaminess, sleaze, and Bohemian flavour of past years. There have been times when this square mile of insalubrious alleys and dark doorways had seemed under threat and, even as I write, developers are waiting to move in and demolish Paul Raymond's landmark revue bar to build a new mega-nightclub (which is after all just what London needs). Let's hope they don't succeed.

Soho seems to have just the right mix of straight and gay, fashionable and exotic, modern and traditional. Girls still stand around, touting outside clubs, beckoning passers-by to enter establishments with such apt names as 'Illusions' and 'Mirage'. I venture in and am accosted twice for money on the way down the precarious stairs to a rank-smelling basement. Two hundred pounds it cost me to watch a tired Eastern European stripper with cellulite and badly fitting rubber knickers waggle her flabby arse in my general direction while I sipped a scandalously overpriced 'house' cocktail.

I walk down Green Court past the porn shop and club joint I worked in for a brief time in the late seventies which is now a hip record shop.

The brothel on Meard Street where I was 'pissed at eleven

in the morning' and we filmed Soft Cell's first video release is now a fashionable clothing shop and next to it is an Asian restaurant.

The Piano Bar has become a new gay bar called Escape, which sounds appropriate enough to me, and next to it is Madame JoJo's, which now hosts a night called Electric GoGo, its electro-clash event. Other, similar clubs – Nag-NagNag, The Cock, Kashpoint – are all within walking distance. Mixed crowds walk past: gay and straight, new hedonists with their own soundtracks and their own super-star DJs: Tasty Tim, Princess Julia, Punx Soundcheck, Johnny Slut and Phil OK. Actually, I DJ at some of these clubs myself from time to time, so maybe I am still part of Soho after all, goddammit.

A few of the old strip clubs have been taken over by clubs celebrating the new burlesque. Yes, burlesque is back with its titillation, temptation and tease, and it sort of feels right for these dark times with its antidote of exotic glamour. It was reinvented for the new millennium, sort of. The reigning queen of burlesque is the American-based Dita Von Teese. Watching her perform at a party in London for the jaded glitterati and fashionista, I was captivated and thrilled by her poise, grace and near perfection. With porcelain skin and raven hair, she soaps off bubbles in a bath after tantiliz-ingly peeling off a tightly laced basque and delicate gloves. The jaded crowd rise to their feet, applaud and whistle, reanimated by something other than cocaine and booze, discovering for a brief moment that they hadn't quite seen it all, before settling back down convinced they just had. And watching a burlesque striptease if you're gay at least gives you an opportunity to admire the intricate lacing and exquis-ite bugle beading on the beautifully constructed costumes.

•

I only recently remembered those days with Frederick. I found myself delving into the past, memories all but forgotten from those days of long petrol-station lines, being woken by the clattering bin collectors just before dawn, the screams and laughter of the prostitutes fighting beneath the Soho window, or the showgirls changing costumes in their dressing rooms above the revue.

They were great times in Soho then but now I live in Bermondsey, south London. In many ways the move is sort of apt, as Bermondsey has always had a salubrious sexual history, especially around London Bridge, Tower Bridge, and beyond, where brothels, bawdy inns and dens of iniquity flourished for centuries; on the east side across from Tower Bridge are the opium dens of Limehouse. It is of course where Oscar Wilde took himself and his character Dorian Gray to mingle with the dissolute.

Walking around the arches and narrow streets around Southwark Cathedral and the Clink Prison, you can still sense the ghosts of the syphilitic whores in their white make-up, rouged cheeks and red bow lips, cleavage bobbling, sucking on a clay pipe and hissing, 'Looking for a good time, guvnor?' Well, you can imagine it if you try hard enough. It is the Dickensian side of London that I love the most, and one that still pervades the mood and architecture of south central and east London. The area from Southwark across to Whitechapel down to Limehouse and back across to Rotherhithe are amazing – the sights, walks, the places to go. You can wander around the streets where Jack the Ripper prowled in Commercial Street, drink in the Ten Bells, and see prostitutes even today ply their trade as did their countless predecessors. The traditional East End strip pubs around Shoreditch across to Bow are still thriving, where buxom lasses tantalizingly remove stockings and fling gar-

ters, while forcing grinning customers' faces into their cleav-
ages. And then there are the pubs where the jukeboxes play
Max Bygraves, Lonnie Donegan and the Beverley Sisters,
and regulars have their own engraved tankards behind the
bar.

On Commercial Road towards the Limehouse end is the
infamous public house, the White Swan, a traditional gay
establishment that holds a notorious amateur strip night
every Wednesday, where young (and not so young) East End
lads get up on stage. Coaxed by alcohol, friends and an
old-fashioned drag queen with a single-entendre name (and
equally lame retorts) they strip to the full monty for a £100
prize. The downside of this of course is the assault by the
baying audience, the humiliation, the intimidating comments
by the drag host about the size of their equipment and the
travesty of the performance. Not long after they begin most
of them realize £100 doesn't seem very much money at all.
It's cruel, loud and pure East End Dickensian Bacchanalia.

Just around the corner, and in complete contrast, is an
infamous East End members-only club, gay too, but at quite
the opposite end of the market. It is a leather-fetish strict
dress code gay club, catering to the more discerning client.
A typical night may well have a veritable array of perverts
who specialize in such exacting fetishes it leaves you quite
bemused: black leather or rubber forms the strict dress code
– no exceptions. The door policy forbids the wearing of
designer label or casual leather, and absolutely no cologne.
Providing you meet this criteria you can explore your fetish
fully, with extremes such as the addition of leather masks,
harnesses, restrictive gags, gas masks and even a metal diving
helmet, or workman's hard hat, through to human ponies,
saddled and bridled, horsehair tails attached to inserted butt
plugs who stand at the bar neighing and nuzzling customers

who feed them sugar lumps; or clients who walk around, genitals exposed, with a catheter inserted and attached to tubes leading to urine container hip flasks. It takes all sorts.

The atmosphere is more early eighties New York than the East End of London.

This extreme fetish bar is one of a kind, but there are numerous other bars and pubs that allow sex on the premises, many quite blatantly, others less so. Near where I live there is a bar; let's call it 'The Castle' to protect the guilty. There is absolutely no doubt what this place is when you enter through its dark portal. The only light source is from the bar, the rest of it is half-lit gloom. Music from a ghetto blaster pumps distorted trance and disco. A row of steel lockers line one room where you can leave your coat, on some nights you must undress entirely. Shadowy figures shuffle from shadowy corners. On certain nights of the week the dress code is underpants only, on other nights the dress code (or should that be undress code) is boots only – literally. Modesty has no place on these nights. At the back of the bar is a large dark room that serves no other purpose than to encourage sex. Basically it's a nightly orgy with a bar.

People arrive, quickly buy a drink and shuffle into the backroom, rarely to be seen until closing time – it often seems there must be a void in the darkness that sucks them in, lost forever. I saw some dubious types disappear into the darkness. It wouldn't be unfair to say the clientele of this particular bar are, on the whole, reminiscent of unlicensed minicab drivers. Occasionally an attractive guy might visit – and once in the back room is pounced upon and devoured. The toilet adjoins the back room, and it too is in semi-darkness, forcing you to feel your way to the doorless cubicle, only to find someone sitting down waiting to get pissed on. The floor is awash with piss and your shoes stick to it, the soles getting tacky as you walk. Then there is the smell that knocks you back – a sour sickly odour of sweat, cigarettes, stale urine, amyl nitrate and something else, a sort of upper bowel excremental odour (don't ask). It seems part of the appeal of this bar is that it is never cleaned, and that seems to add, for some gay men, to the intoxication of it. Gay sex bars are on the whole dark, dank, dirty places where strangers can indulge in anonymous sexual encounters, though the reality is that almost everyone knows everyone else, and no one is that anonymous. The gay sex scene is relatively small, and the chances are that everyone is only one encounter short of having sex with everyone else.

Midweek is Slave Training night, and every third Monday early evening is Potty Training. Look, it takes all sorts. If any of this sounds like your sort of thing, it is worth a visit. What I'm saying is that London has changed, and for the better.

Of the other bars I've visited in South London, and there are quite a few, one stands out in particular. It was the first underpants party I went to. My friend called me up and dared me to go with him. Naturally I was reluctant at first, but curiosity won over modesty and I agreed. It was held at a pub situated in the middle of a Peckham housing estate, the last place in the world you'd expect it. Clothes had to be checked at the door and placed in a black bag, leaving you standing in only your underpants and boots. I felt self-conscious but somewhat liberated.

Since that occasion I have visited several other such parties, the only awkward moments occurring when you bump into someone you know. You see, everyone wants to be there but no one wants anyone they know to know they go there, if you get my drift. So you pretend not to see them and they you, and you move in different directions, having established an unspoken rule between you. It's all part of the strange behavioural ritual played out at such places. I always think it is a great shame such nights don't generally exist for heterosexuals. Perhaps this is because the sexual politics between men and women are far too complicated and fragile for such chance encounters and misinterpretations. The few straight sex clubs or nights that do exist have to be bound up in so many house rules, including discouraging singles, and allowing only consenting mixed couples.

In my final short exploration of London sex nights, one club I couldn't resist visiting is the Club Asshole. Ring on the doorbell and enter into not so much a club as someone's living room, furnished in white plastic garden furniture (moulded), with a TV in the corner showing seventies porno. Two elderly gents dressed in sun shorts and flip-flops snatch your £5 admission and put your coat in a plastic bag. As no alcohol is on sale (this really has an air of a private party), you can bring your own bottle and they'll stick it in the fridge. Then it's downstairs to the cellar, a collection of adjoining rooms where customers creep around. The cellar is eerily silent, the only sound the muffle of the video playing upstairs. The lighting is provided by dim reproduction Victorian carriage lights (candle bulbs flicker) hanging off the mouldy walls. Occasionally you hear the pad pad of footsteps as shadowy figures move through the rooms, the unzipping of trouser flies, the grunt or moan from a corner. As your eyes gradually grow accustomed to the darkness you become aware of more and more people; tonight about twenty or so skulk around. An elderly man leads a handsome youth on a lead, encouraging others to have sex with him. Another couple have brought an inflatable lilo on which they perform sex acts with each other in full view of everyone. All these acts are performed in relative silence. At the furthest end of the cellar is a final room, no more than a coal-hole-cum-dungeon in which three of the most emaciated dead-eyed men perform sex acts on each other – expressionless and dispassionate, and certainly not safe. I look on at this display of Grand Guignol grotesquerie. I suspect that I have finally reached the lower colon of London's bowels, the final circle of a pleasureless Hell as they sodomize and beat the leering drooling receptacle that lies motionless on the floor. Like some illustration from Dante's Inferno, they have sunk about as low as you can go, which is not a moral judgement but a fact. This is physical sex and nothing else: anonymous, silent, extreme and unfulfillable. Gradually, over time, the boundaries of the physical are extended; what began as a finger eventually becomes a fist, a slap becomes a punch, then even that won't be enough. The depths to which people can sink is astonishing, but as I was to discover these weren't as low as it went, not by a long way.

I expelled myself from the bowels of the club in need of a beauty fix and shower – at least I knew why it was called Club Asshole. Actually, I discovered I had changed: years ago I would have rushed out and written a song about it, whereas now I've written a chapter about it. Similar scenes in the New York club Hellfire had a profound experience on my work. But it seems I have changed. Now I look for something life-changing and inspiring – such places make me feel unimpassioned. Perhaps I've seen it all too many times and in better surroundings, but it's as joyless as ever. On the whole I've come to realize that S&M clubs are not for me, despite the misconception that I'm an aficionado of them. How many articles have that headline about me being the "Perverted Pixie of Pop" Marc Almond [insert age], who likes to dress in rubber and leather, and wield a whip . . .' This stems from early in my career when I took journalists to such iniquitous places, wrote songs like 'Sex Dwarf', 'Seedy Films' and 'Baby Doll', cavorted around in videos wearing a harness and bondage outfits and threatened hacks with bull whips. So in hindsight I might have sent out mixed signals but it was just about trying to shock; I wasn't really into that S&M scene. I always remained on the periphery of it, fascinated by the secret world it created and the influences it gave me.

•

Calling our album *Non Stop Erotic Cabaret* and recording it in New York drew the scene to us as the downtown freaks showed us the underbelly of the city and life imitated art. Dave and I were from art school and loved performance art, and, let's face it, some of these things you see in S&M clubs aren't that different from performance art pieces.

Where was I? S&M, not for me. I found it interesting, I suppose, in a provincial middle-class kind of way: unconventional, risqué, alternative. But now I've come to realize that it's a right old rigmarole, especially the kind of S&M where they don't actually have sex. It's like an hour of foreplay and nothing else. It's a lot of posturing, nipple-tweaking, pushing and shoving, buckling and unbuckling, and empty promises. Like I said, it is performance art and not actually sex, and I'm glad it exists and that people go to such extraordinary lengths to do it, but it is just not my bag.

Of course between the extremes there are numerous offerings for those prepared to look and travel, and I discovered that it's not all hopeless. Let me tell you about a good time I had that restored some of my faith that my journey was not futile. It happened not so long ago when I was desperately trying to dredge up some exciting situations to share with you. A swingers party. It took place in Croydon, that less than glamorous suburb of London, though recently touted by its council in a press release as the new New York.

A friend of mine insisted I go, securing an invite from the more than accommodating hosts. The party took place in an unassuming semi-detached council house with a well-manicured garden. My hosts, whom I shall call Barbara and Ron, obviously had a great deal of pride in their home and, as I was to discover from Ron, had purchased it under the Conservatives' 'own your council house scheme' of the mid-eighties. I arrived as instructed at 6.30 p.m. for a prompt 7.00 p.m. start. Latecomers would not be admitted, I was informed. Barbara met me at the door and ushered me quickly inside, before peeping out to check no one had noticed my clandestine arrival, or the neighbours her lace-up latex ensemble, including a floor-length pearlized pink latex skirt. I tried to imagine how long she had spent cramming herself into her latex outfit: rolls of fat billowing over every hem, her waist painfully nipped and eschewed by a tight belt. She reminded me of one of those saucy seaside postcards I used to see in Southport: 'Have you seen my little Willy?'

She took my coat. 'The marvellous thing about our parties,' she whispered, while looking somewhat disapprovingly at my attire (or lack of effort I had made), 'is that we hold them on Saturdays – no one has to worry about work and Saturday night television isn't what it used to be.'

The hallway was painted in a strange blue colour, the lighting flat from a white bulb, and the overall effect was cold and stark. Ron came into the hall and shook my hand, leading me through to the lounge. I sat on the sofa which was covered in clear plastic, I suspected to protect the velveteen fabric. I could hear them muttering to each other in the hall. The lounge was dominated by a fake-flame gas fire with imitation brick surround, the room bare of personal effects. It needed enlivening but I was sure that would happen later. Looking around, those three little words came to mind – Bowen, Llewellyn and Laurence. I could imagine Carol Smiley stapling fake zebra skin pelmets over the curtains and stencilled Botticelli cupids fluttering around the walls.

On a coffee table were a selection of pretzels and crisps, dips including livid pink taramasalata and phosphorescent green guacamole, and a glass bowl filled with condoms and sachets of lube. Rolls of kitchen towels, tissues and a jar of Nutella spread completed the offering. I suddenly imagined faces looking up from fleshy crevices smeared with Nutella and deep tongue-kissing after a dip in the taramasalata. What is it with straight people and food/sex? All that was missing was the proverbial fruit and whipped cream dispenser. Mushy fruit and souring cream would play havoc with the carpet, mind, and it looked like an expensive shag pile too. Not to mention the bedding considerations.

Barbara made a drink, vodka tonic, second-guessing it was what I drank and I, too polite to decline it, thanked her. Other guests began to arrive, making their way upstairs in turn to change into their evening wear. Barbara seemed in her element – she was on. Plonking a swizzle stick in my drink she stepped back and sized me up. What would interest me? I could see her mind ticking over, cogs and wheels lubricated by Dubonnet and lemon. Now people were mingling about in the lounge, drinking and flirting. A couple quizzically eyed me up, a woman in a basque had a thousand questions she wanted to ask me (you could see it in the eyes) but dared not, guessing that I wanted to retain some anonymity. Barbara had earlier banned Ron (within earshot) from playing 'Tainted Love', so I figured I could relax for now.

Then, just before 7 p.m., the star couple arrived – I guess they were the star couple, the centrepiece of the party, because everyone was clearly excited by their arrival and also because they were a good few years younger than anyone else there. They had firm bodies, outfits that were not too outré and if you squinted from the other side of the room through your drink they looked not unattractive. No, that's unfair: in the present company they were stunners.

Barbara sat on the edge of the sofa by me, reached into a make-up bag, squinted into a compact mirror and examined the fine lines around her mouth and the slackening muscles around her eyes. She then painted a lighter blue on the dark blue of her eyelids, a darker red outlining the pale red of her lips. It seemed it was all a question of light and shade.

She eyed me seductively and kissed a red wrinkled oval into a white tissue, found it too secret, too sexual to discard, and slipped it into her make-up bag. Ron returned from upstairs, walking in naked. Barbara looked at him, then cast a glance at me with an expression of 'Well, what do you think of him then?'

Ron put on a Burt Bacharach CD and mingled.

> What do you get when you fall in love?
> A guy with a pin to burst your bubble.

Guests helped themselves to nibbles whilst fondling each other. A hawkish woman was being fed a crisp seductively, salt and crumbs sticking on the lipstick in the corner of her mouth. Then Ron sat beside me and struck up a conversation, telling me about his job as a lathe operator, about their now fortnightly parties, the extent of the swinging scene, and how he met like-minded people by advertising in *Loot*, which I thought in this Internet age was still quite quaint. 'Versatile couples with unusual interests seek like minded – Croydon area' was the sort of thing I imagined. Then he told me about their house rules (which struck me as somewhat late in the day). He never shut up. How he had been at one particular party and a well-known ex-soap star had been at it in front of all and sundry: 'You'd be surprised about the celebrities that are into the scene,' he said, tapping his nose and winking. 'Household names!'

By now the party was in full swing, the star couple enjoying foreplay with each other on the shag, intent on putting on a floor show.

At one point Ron brought over an object for me to examine, to guess its purpose. It was a small (around twelve inches long) wheeled trolley that sat about four inches off the floor, made out of natural cherry wood, though dark cherry was available too, Ron informed me. Barbara returned and stood over us, encouraging me to hazard a guess.

Confounded, I gave up.

Ron leaned over me, his stomach thankfully covering his flaccid member, and announced it was a slipper valet.

Barbara elaborated. 'For storing your slippers on.'

'Oh, right,' I said, utterly perplexed that such an object even existed.

I suddenly found myself hemmed in by both of them. Barbara began stroking my hair, Ron coaxingly fondling his penis between his thumb and index finger. Earlier Ron had confessed to me that he was forty-five years old (going on sixty-five, I guessed), but if true that made me one of the oldest people there. So why did I feel they were akin to my parents? Was I on the outside looking in or vice versa? What had happened to me? One minute in life I'm rushing on ecstasy, snorting cocaine, a fervid sexual outlaw and club fiend, and the next thing you know I'm in a Croydon living room trying to think of excuses to fend off the advances of two oversexed suburbanites.

Life, what the hell do you make of it?

Looking around me at everyone copulating, my mind wandered to the plans for the following Sunday. A friend was making a roast chicken dinner with all the trimmings, followed by pear crumble. I noticed a man ejaculate over a woman's breasts. It would be great, I thought, if my friend had Carnation milk for the crumble.

Barbara and Ron stood up and made their way to the hallway that led upstairs to, I guessed, their bedroom. Barbara hesitated, returned and whispered in my ear, 'We'll be upstairs, no rush.'

I saw Ron standing in the doorway. He winked at me, before disappearing. Barbara quickly followed.

I sat for a moment taking in the furnishings, and then moved over to the window and looked out. The patio outside at the back had a border of ivy which was quite springy and prosperous, and made me suspicious that, like the curtains in the lounge, it might be counterfeit.

Finding my coat in the kitchen I quietly slipped away. I felt it was less rude than spurning their advances would have been, and I was sure they would understand.

•

On my way back into London, I thought about Barbara and Ron, and how we all make our own personal pleasure palaces. It seems I too might find mine, perhaps by discovering what I didn't want and working backwards from there. Since I never intended to be this old, I needed to look on my age as a new beginning. I first needed to lay to rest some old ghosts, and that meant returning to an old haunt that held many memories. Where am I talking about? New York of course: if you can't find it there you can't find it anywhere.

5

New York

I still love New York

•

I felt the familiar thrill building up as the plane touched down at JFK. The alluring red horizon and the muted lights of Queens, the shimmering sparkle of the runway lamps. My sore eyes reddened from the cabin pressure, stale air and watching a TV screen just that bit too small. Blurring all that confusion of light added disorientation to the apprehension and excitement. After navigating the nightmare that is US customs I moved out into the chill evening air. Would I still be inspired by New York? Would it help me make sense of my midlife crisis, provide any answers? Probably not, but the trip's paid for.

London may be beautiful and mysterious, steeped in history, elegant, confused, majestic, et cetera, but it was hard to argue against the claim that New York is the greatest city in the world. Is or was? So many possibilities at my fingertips, New York has always been a second home for me. I love so much about it, from the taxi ride into Manhattan when you arrive, the skyline looming up in front of you until it consumes you, like a row of sequinned giants, almost threatening, daring you not to be awestruck; and without fail my jaw always drops and I can barely suppress a gasp.

Mountains of concrete and glass against a sky of congo blue and aquamarine. The Empire State building, erotic and proud, lit in seasonal colours, once more the unchallenged king of New York. Since 11 September, I still find myself looking for the iconic towers, even though I had seen the footage on TV replayed at the flimsiest of excuses, over and over. I remember, as my New York friend Darren sat on my sofa in London on the day it happened, I cried in disbelief, unable to clearly locate the source of my emotional outpouring. And still in New York I look for the Twin Towers, expecting them to appear any minute as you turn a corner: seeing the view from Sheridan Square on 7th Avenue looking downtown, lit up at night, standing guard somewhere at the far end of town; or sunbathing on Christopher Street pier, as the New Jersey yahoos sped past in the boats shouting insults, and there they were, defiant silver monoliths, glistening and glowering. Now it seems like forever ago.

I always feel so afraid on every return that the city would have changed beyond recognition. As much as I might fight in the corner for change I really want things to stay the same. Like a blind person reaching for a familiar past, I want to feel secure in a life where more often than not I feel the opposite. I'll go to a city, visit the same places, the same restaurants, sit at the same table and eat the same thing on the menu. I rush from pillar to post, my heart beating, hoping that a cherished spot is still there.

I wanted to know New York's dark in the shadows. To know that its underbelly was still there would be enough for me. And all would be well in the world. There was something about being in its wide avenues, whether in the humid sexy summer heat or the bracing winter cold, that brought words and melodies to mind.

·

The first thing I discovered was that porn movies can no longer be shown. Can you believe that? No porno movies in New York? And porn videos can only be sold in stores that agree to stock 60 per cent regular videos. How stupid is that? Wouldn't you think that it would draw people into the store who might otherwise not go into a porn store – 'Now where's that video of *Annie* stocked? But hey, what's this at the back, *Anal Tushy*?' Peep-o-Rama, a rundown sex store in the heart of Manhattan, was awkwardly sandwiched between a souvenir shop and 'Tad's Broiled Steaks'. This 24-hour 'adult centre', with its one-dollar video booths, had been the final holdout against the Disneyfication of 42nd Street and Times Square. The lease finally ran out and money finally proved more than a match for nostalgia.

Various clean-up campaigns came and went, but the smut storeowners finally met their match in Mayor Rudolph Giuliani. The enforcement of strict zoning laws governing sex-related businesses, combined with high real estate prices, slowly ousted the smut clubs one by one. Even the last remaining strip bars had to remove the word 'Topless' from signs and hoardings. Bars that specialized in bare-breasted go-go dancers such as Billy's Topless got round this for a while by shifting the 's' across until it read 'Billy Stopless'. I love New Yorkers – inventive survivors. All the porno cinemas have gone, turned into cheap food restaurants. Just what New York needs.

On arriving in the city I checked into my favourite hotel, the Gramercy Park, situated on Lexington Avenue and 14th. Great location, an attractive part of the city looking across New York's last remaining private park, the hotel has old-world charm. It was where Humphrey Bogart married Helen Menken in 1926, and where a rowdy Babe Ruth was once thrown out. It needs charm because the service is terrible, room service has all but ceased and the bar no longer has a tinkling piano. Everything changed after one of the owners committed suicide by jumping off the roof, landing on the pavement in front of arriving guests. So tragic but so New York. Still it soldiers on and at least the new TVs in the rooms now worked. Mine just repeated the words 'War on Terror' and 'War on Iraq'. Was there a war on?

More worrying were the news reports that 'the government' wants to monitor your emails and arrest you without reason and convict you without trial. The land they call free is in danger of losing its proud moniker. The United States is slowly eroding its citizens' personal freedoms, brought about by a combination of new technologies, laws that do not respect privacy and companies seeking ever-wider knowledge of their customers. Americans have noticed that they are heading for a future in which every move is monitored, every financial transaction recorded and every interaction with other people noted and analysed. The information will be used by the FBI to look for terrorists, the police to look for criminals – and McDonald's to sell them more hamburgers.

American news is too depressing. It is so localized unless there is an international crisis involving their country, and even then it manages to come up with stories somehow relating to the international angle: 'Manhattan Women Knit Quilts For Marines', 'New Yorkers Hold Vigil For Marines' or 'Brooklyn Marine Gets Hero's Welcome'.

There was without doubt a feeling of malaise. But like a sick at heart old lady searching for the man who never comes, New York lifts her face towards the flattering light, injects her collagen, applies a little too much make-up, pats her overfed, overbred dog, locks the door and struts down 5th Avenue to face the world.

Once on the street a familiar feeling of anticipation that something was going to happen overwhelmed me, the sort of thing that will affect your life. New York does that. Leaving the hotel is fraught with the unexpected, an adventure each time. It is always good to adopt a streetwise demeanour, like you are meant to be there and, like most New Yorkers, just a little nutty.

First I checked out my favourite video store, a brief cab ride up to 8th and 34th to the Triple XXX. Now being away from Times Square these stores are of little interest to developers and the city, and as yet remain open for business. Stumbling across the place one day years ago I was amazed that the upstairs male section was lined with big black guys and Puerto Rican hustlers, all tattoos and gold teeth, streetwise gaits and baggy clothes, winking and grinning and tugging on what looked like truncheons in their sports track pants (all right, you get the picture). Some of them would even flip their nightsticks out for a moment, lewd yet proud. The most common phrase was, 'What's up?'

Two guys sat at either side of the booths changing dollars (you need to have single dollar bills to feed into the porn movie screens that play inside the booths that line each wall). It didn't take me long to twig that these guys could turn a blind eye for $5 and not see you slip one of the hard-selling hustlers into a booth with you (one person in a booth at a time was the normal rule).

'Keep moving, keep spending, no loitering,' the attendants would shout at the non-moving, non-spending, loitering throng. Dollars were fed into the slots inside the booth to keep the red light flashing outside – as long as the light kept flashing outside the hustler could keep flashing inside. By 6 p.m. the place would be packed with the businessmen shift. Lots of shuffling, whispering, dealing, pretending to look at the videos on display, followed by a quick slip into a booth. All these hustlers would claim they were straight, all with money-hungry girlfriends in Brooklyn, even a kid or two; either that or Mr Crackman was waiting impatiently on the corner to whisk them away.

But all that was then, and now on this visit things have changed. It was a wasteland, just a couple of confused hustlers wandering in and out and a lone frustrated customer (no, not me) who hadn't cottoned on to what was not happening. I asked the dreadlocked attendant, who must have seen it all, what happened. When the old mayor passed the baton to the new mayor (Giuliani to Bloomberg) everything relaxed; for a while, business boomed. But it was not to last. Apparently a Puerto Rican hustler had slipped into a booth with a plain-clothes cop – not exactly a honey trap, more a tar pit. Bang! Not literally, and it was the final warning for the XXX. The owner had been on his umpteenth caution and was petrified his business would be closed altogether. Time to clean the place up. 'Guys, keep moving, no loitering, we MEAN it!!!' Outside on the street a hustler informed me that trade had moved to the Playpen on 8th and 42nd Street. They always move somewhere, you just had to know where.

I took a walk up to 44th. The Playpen. The Playpen is notable for being the former Cameo. A close inspection reveals two female figures above the door, one holding a film canister and the other, a camera. The neon sign still shows the Twin Towers. With a colourful and lurid past it had once been the famous burlesque stripper Gypsy Rose Lee's own theatre. Gypsy Rose Lee, the legendary woman who told the police during a raid at the famous Minsky's burlesque house, 'I wasn't naked. I was completely covered by a blue spotlight,' was known as 'the most publicized woman in the world'. She was one of the most famous strippers of all time. That was a long time ago. In its most recent incarnation the Playpen had been the successor to the notorious Adonis Lounge – never quite capturing the grotty green velvet charm of the original, but on its repainted walls you could still see the odd adornment of its Gypsy Rose past buried beneath. Now as the Playpen it was a shell, with peep booths, video cabins and shelves of porno videos. Ramshackle, dirty, gone was the tease, in came the sleaze. It had become a desperate whore on its last legs, squeezing those final dollars, only a matter of time before the redevelopers knocked on its doors. Upstairs in the male section was a line of booths; outside each stood a hustler, the Times Square variety, down at heel, worn out and tired, mainly addicts prepared to do anything for enough cash for their next fix. Not a lot of joy here. The same old attendant on the same old scam grinned at me.

The Big Apple, the dollar whore
Ripens round a rotten core.

•

Moving on to where the Show Palace Theater had stood, just along 8th Avenue from the corner of 42nd Street. No sign it had ever been there. Now there is an ugly multiplex cinema. On the opposite corner stands the Port Authority bus terminal, where the fresh-faced, well-fed farm boys had first arrived off Greyhound buses, in search of adventure, stardom, a taste of something other than the small town life. Money, love, fame – can't get that at home. Most had not got any further than the corner of 42nd Street. Look, even now if you stand and take the time, you can see them, ghosts of young men loitering, out too late, trying to blend into the crowd. Like everyone else they pretend to ignore the tall big-haired transvestite hooker with high high heels and long legs screaming and voguing across the street; gaunt youths desperate, all that apple pie and corn bread long sucked out of them by the vampires that prowl the corner.

Most of the bars where they would have turned a few dollars, kept warm, and maybe met an understanding stranger (meaning generous) for the night, or at least a half hour – places like the Savoy, Trix, Cats – (though now relocated) were all now closed. I remember it was a night of mourning the evening they loaded the entire cast of customers of the bar Cats into a meat wagon and whisked them all away, banging down the shutters – 'Closed by Order of the City'.

The bar Cats – a thinly veiled disguise as a pre- and post-theatre bar for Andrew Lloyd Webber musical aficionados – lasted as long as the musical it shared the block with, but its time came to an end at the same time as the musical, 'Memories'. Legend has it that Dee Dee Ramone was discovered there.

There were still a couple of bars around the 53rd Street area but they were for upmarket hustlers, the ones who accompany punters to the theatre, a meal. Some, so I've heard on good authority, are even capable of holding a passable conversation.

•

Down 42nd Street I did something I always wanted to do: I took a room in the Elk Hotel (360 West 42nd Street), a short stay hotel – meaning you can rent a room for anything up to four hours. I just wanted to sit for a while in one of its many box-like rooms looking out onto 42nd Street. I tied back the curtains and let the flickering neon light up the room. In the corner was a small sink, soap and towel, and a double bed covered in an off-grey fitted sheet. Close inspection wasn't recommended. I sat and listened to the sounds,

soaking in the atmosphere – giggles, shrieks, banging, muf-
fled conversations (the walls have the paper thinness of a
motel in an Elroy Leonard novel) and people having hurried
sex. Outside car horns punctuated the soundtrack of daily
life, vendors shouting, dealers arguing. It was all too cinematic. How many sexual encounters had taken place in this
room, how many grubby dollars had changed hands, dirty
needles shared? How much semen had spattered the walls,
the carpet, for sure the curtains? The past and present
mingled, the voices of the lustful and violent heard clearest.

Outside on the corner stands Show World, battle hardened, thumbing its nose defiantly at city regulations. It
somehow manages to exist outside restricted boundaries and
its owner refuses to sell. They (City Hall) have tried to wear
it down and it had to stop its peep shows and one-on-one
encounter booths. This place is a huge complex with multiple
floors. Depending on what side you enter from, it's hard to
figure out how many floors it really is. At least three. Back
in the early eighties, they had live sex shows and I remember
going there into the 'Kinky Room' to see a feature and she
did three or four guys sitting in the front.

Today, the features do a little audience participation but
nothing compared to the good old days. There are other
areas with one-on-one peep shows as well as many-to-one
peep booths (a number of peep booths surrounding a circular
stage), where customers slip in a token that prompts a screen
to slide up revealing a girl gyrating in everyone's general
direction). All behind glass of course, like some secret reptile
house. Looking around you could see the transfixed faces,
all looking at her and at each other looking at her as she
poked and preened and removed her panties just as the
token time was up and the screen slid down.

Baby Doll is on her trapeze

•

So Show World, stripped of its one-on-one encounters, still hangs on in there with its video booths, erotic (meaning clothed) dancers, and occasional art performance shows. Soft Cell were recently invited to perform there. Though it never happened it could have easily been the pinnacle of my career. Forget the Albert Hall (which is actually what my agent said), Soft Cell at Show World, now that would have been something.

Just up Broadway is the new Disneyland: renovated ex-porno and B-movie theatres, shoddily resurrected into imitations of cinemas, in much the same style as imitation fifties American diners purport the endorsement of a simple past with the efficiency of present profit margins – fast food joints and souvenir shops vie with each other. Its gaudiness almost appealed to me with its pale neon and contrived delights. Facade with no content. That is so Now. A distraction reflecting entertainment. In the late seventies and early eighties, New York was nastier than nasty. Live boy/girl sex shows on stage were the norm. Strip clubs merged with brothels and vice versa. In fact, things were so crazy, you didn't even have to go to a strip club to see nudity.

But all good things always seem to come to an end. The live sex shows ended in the eighties and alas, as of 1999, the city has even cleaned up Times Square for poor defenceless Disney. Now it's even hard to find a good porno book store, let alone a nasty strip club. But already how quickly it was becoming tarnished and dated. The shadow people and creatures of the night are already drawn to the tourists and the flashing lights. As long as the Port Authority bus terminal remains there, there will always be those to pick off, a never-ending conveyor belt of young Americans.

Over in the corner opposite the bus station stood a black pimp in a white fur coat and matching brimmed hat, cartoon parody, surrounded by his 'Ho's' – a phalanx of hookers. Not long now before another Greyhound bus pulls in.

Not long now before the cheap Disney facades fall apart and the big ol' recession kicks in. Nothing ages. New York is, after all, the gateway to America, so each new mayor needs to at least give it a lick of paint. Times Square is just a bad location, or good, depending on your perversity.

•

When in Manhattan I always look forward to seeing an old friend called Scott Ewalt, an artist and occasional DJ who is also a collector of NY memorabilia and chronicler of all things burlesque, not to mention a friend of the film maker and photographer, the now legendary Jim Bidgood, director of the classic gay erotica movie *Pink Narcissus*.

In 1971, *Pink Narcissus* rocked the underground film world with its dreamlike homoerotic images. A lush, artistic piece of gay erotica about an impossibly handsome young man, obsessed with his own beauty and youth, who escapes the realities of street life through intricately choreographed Walter Mitty-esque fantasies in which he portrays a Roman slave, a matador, a wood nymph, and a harem boy. *Pink Narcissus'* writer and director was credited as 'Anonymous' and it was later revealed that director James Bidgood, a physique photographer, had taken his name off the film because he did not like what the distributor had done with his work. *Pink Narcissus* is reminiscent of Genet's *Un Chant d'Amour* in its obsession with flowers, rough sexuality, and extraordinary male beauty, but it is more like a drag queen's opium-soaked dream version or a Disney adaptation of Genet's work than it is a direct descendant. It is sometimes difficult to discern fantasy from reality in the film.

Jim had now been rediscovered and his work re-evaluated by the German publishing house Taschen, who had published a big gaudy book of stills of his work. We finally met in a local diner and discussed things over a salad. Jim was fabulously jaded yet still brimming with ideas. Now in his seventies he told me his secret to a fulfilled old age: his favourite evenings were spent taking a tab of acid, watching porn videos and indulging himself with a dick pump. Well, you couldn't argue with that, could you?

Anyway, back to my friend Scott. We planned to do a night crawl of sleaze spots in the city just to reassure ourselves that there was still a world worth visiting. Reassure ourselves it was still not time to line up the Nembutals and say kiss my ass and goodbye to life.

We decided to meet at Stella's on 266 West 47th Street, our intention being to get a taste of each place and move on, particularly since I no longer have the staying power compared to the party animal I once was. And my attention threshold is at an all-time low. On my way I passed the boarded-up Trix Bar and felt a pang of nostalgia and sadness. Maybe our memories, those windows to the past, get boarded up too when they can't be relived.

But I was reassured when I arrived at Stella's to find it in full swing, and past memories enveloped me, filling in the gaps that time had faded. It was still there and, in the words of Mae West, 'Taste the Fruit' came to mind. Upstairs at Stella's is the main bar, mostly frequented by Latin hustlers, whilst downstairs is a smoky basement. Throughout the evening a procession of muscular black and Latin guys took turns to strip, peeling off their outfits (which almost always consisted of long black shiny coats with hoods, or wide pimp hats). They are allowed to be almost naked and possess an erection, but only if their penises are sheathed in material – lycra, leather, sequins. This creates a bizarre effect of making their naturally oversized members appear even more obscene. They danced and cavorted, flexed and vogued in an attempt to impress, but one guy did a spectacular trick that overshadowed all the others. Looking like a down-on-his-luck Prince, this guy removed his clothes and lay on a table, manoeuvred his legs behind his head and puckered his anus in and out. And that was his act. New York's a tough city, so whatever talent you have, you better use it.

After the performance (and I use that word lightly) he joined the others and worked the room, mingling with the audience, one on one, urging you to stuff dollar bills into his already overbulging sheath. The generous got a private dance and a close inspection of the sheath's contents. Eventually the room was full of gyrating scantily clad guys hustling for whatever morsels of gratitude were available. The smell of musky sweat and whiff of dope in the air was intoxicating.

Afterwards we walked through Times Square, looking sadly at the restaurants that have replaced the former pleasure palace venues. Past the sites of the former sex cinema Eros, Adonis Lounge and the Capri, all gone. Times Square still dazzles but it is all promise. I stood in the middle, trying to take it all in, agog at the scale of it: millions of lights engulf you, enormous hoardings and neon advertisements encase entire buildings, celebrating the power and scale of capitalism. On the street I watched two jewellery salesmen touting their goods from open suitcases, full of cheap chains. Suddenly they were wrestled to the ground by plain-clothes cops, handcuffed and led away. The trashy jewellery and fake watches scattered across the paving, tourists grasping what they could. Times Square is a wretched place, a shrine to a god that has no compassion or tolerance.

Scott told me he had heard of a new hustler bar down near 53rd Street called Red. You had to know where it was as the flyer didn't reveal the location. Scott of course knew. When we arrived the door was answered by a couple of nervous-looking proprietors; after all, one minute it's hello and the next you could be busted. Upstairs was the lounge. Latin hustlers in shorts were giving back massages in between gyrating on a podium while porno was playing on a couple of TV screens. A reassuring red light illuminated the proceedings. The hustlers had seen better days but they were at least enthusiastic. The place was not very full but then that comes from not advertising the address. Yet within weeks of our visit I learned it had been raided, the hustlers clothed and shown the door. The reason I mention Red is because it is so typical of New York – open up, grab what you can and try to stay one step ahead of the authorities. It's this constant change that makes it so edgy; it felt like a city on cocaine, chasing some elusive high. I began to suspect it might not be the best place to find some way out of my midlife crisis

We called by the Cock for a quick drink. The Cock is a bar located at 12th Street and Avenue A, and has, in case you somehow missed it while passing, a big red cock in the window. A rooster of course. Scott DJs there on a Thursday to a downtown friendly crowd, cruisy and sleazy. I took a seat and Doug, the ex-editor of *Honcho* magazine, joined us. Doug was accompanied by a young man who proceeded to tell us how he loves to collect urine in jars until in crystallizes. Why he does that is anybody's guess. I simply hold an expression of 'isn't that fascinating'.

Then out of the blue Doug ordered him to show me his

cock – he was a model of Scott's and apparently it was a
beauty, and he loved exhibiting it. After much masturbating
and wangling in an attempt to coax it to attention he gave
up, blaming too much alcohol. I took his word for it. The
Cock used to be much raunchier with a heaving back room,
de rigueur for any self-respecting gay bar in those days.
But like everywhere else in New York at the end of the
millennium, it too was raided. Drug dealing in the corner
and the fact that a couple got carried away and copulated in
the window one night didn't help matters. There are always
some to spoil it for the rest.

In those early days there were also performances, which
either involved people masturbating and/or firing objects out
of their anus. That was then. Now only go-go dancers stand
on the bar and dangle over the oblivious customers. When
Ivan 'the lonely go-go dancer' is dancing it's always something special. He featured in one of my New York shows
and now is in demand as a porno actor and appears in
such well-known titles as *Staten Island Sex Cult*, for which
I supplied two songs.

We left the Cock and went across to a fashionable new
club a couple of blocks away called Opaline, a hip mixed
crowd, dancing to the latest electro clash sounds. A selection
of downtown doyens and art types lingered around, looking unimpressed and 'so' bored, a look New Yorkers have
perfected. Despite the changes New Yorkers can still make
the effort to be bored, and the club scene, which is directly
descended from those early clubs like Mudd and Danceteria
in the early eighties, just fails to excite any of them.

The club is hosted by the formidable Mistress Formika, a
living cornerstone of that other legendary Trash Rock club
from the early nineties, Squeezebox, that spawned the legendary Hedwig of the Angry Inch fame. Mistress Formika is
one of the New York stalwart survivors who always reinvent

themselves, see a niche and fill it. You can't keep them down for long. New York is a tough town with so much going against the artier, edgier subversives. Despite the rising rent spaces and the moral clean-ups, it is great to know that so many familiar faces are at Opaline, still bursting with creativity.

Our last port of call had to be the club Esquelita, the infamous Latin Drag Club on 39th and 8th, where, as a wide-eyed northern boy visiting New York over twenty years earlier, I felt I had found a magical pleasure palace. But first, even back then, you have to find the damn place. It's in that nether zone of warehouses and non-gentrified dwellings in the West 30s. Line-waiting time is mandatory and nobody gets round it. Once inside imagine a run-down casino with an 'Evening of Tango Madness' revue as recreated by acid-casualty drag queens with unlimited access to the sequin-and-feathers. Like a Mexican theme chain restaurant, Esquelita leans heavily on salsa kitsch to draw the crowds, and ironically Latino authentico is often the flavour least evident. Elegant dramatic divas in diaphanous spangled gowns and coiffed wigs, glittering tattooed arms outstretched à la Bassey, perfectly lip-synching to Spanish ballads, while a family audience circled the dance floor, showing respect and appreciation in equal measure by shoving dollars down the front of the performers' dresses as they work the room. They didn't miss a beat, even when stopping to retrieve tips that had loosened and fallen, maintaining their elegance the utmost priority – certainly money mattered but the illusion was all. The dirty dollar seemed almost beneath them, exalted and elevated by the spectacle.

My favourite had been one of the divas who arrived as a man with fake beard and seventies hair wig, polyester shirt and tie, and mimed to a ballad by Julio Iglesias. Halfway through the song he began to remove his clothes, then the beard (careful not to spoil the make-up underneath). Before our eyes he changed sex, as too did the song, from a man's vocal to a woman's. At a climactic key change, the outfit, velcroed, was ripped away, the wig pulled off, releasing a mane of blonde hair, a wind machine blowing out the tresses and the folds of the sequinned gown – a perfect cinematic moment of orgasmic climax. Such was the perfection of the execution, that dollars rained down, acolytes worshipped and I had an epiphany. I remember thinking it was one of the most exciting things I had seen.

It was a million miles away from the misogynistic British impersonators, especially the northern drag I knew, ugly and clumsy and berating, a sad comedy panto kind of approach with the usual pathetic retorts about . . . well, you can guess. But the drag in New York was a celebration of women, elegant, powerful, larger than life women – women they knew and who were real. Divas with attitude that ruled a world where men were mere slavish mortals – that sort of thing. I wrote a song, inspired and named after that club – Esquelita.

The club itself is situated in a slightly dodgy part of 8th Avenue where hookers, pimps and the whiff of crack fill the sidewalks – it's not a place to loiter. The club had changed very little, the entrance switching to round the corner, and of course over the years it had moved in and out of fashion. But that night, all those years later, I entered and felt something of the wide-eyed thrill I'd felt all those years ago. Then I knew New York wasn't over. Hell! It was still alive and well in the bowels of Esquelita. A tribal dance track pounded out, all primitive drums and sweaty passion. Inside semi-naked dancers gyrated on podiums, girls knelt before them simulating fellatio, eneveloped by red lights and thick smoke; Latino queens, black hustlers, fag hags and drag queens all vied for space and attention.

When the show finally started at 2.30 I was almost ready to leave – I came, I tasted, I danced, I faded. But I was glad I decided to hang on. Out on to the dance floor walked a leggy drag queen to host the evening's entertainment; after a disco dancing lip-synch she embarked on her repartee with the audience: put-down followed by retort, the audience were playing into her hands – 'giving shade', I think it's called.

But then one loud-mouthed queen went too far and the host called security over. What happened next was a little unclear but after introducing the next act (and God forbid if it wasn't the black-coated Prince lookalike with the talented arsehole we'd seen earlier at Stella's) all hell broke loose. An almighty fight ensued, tables thrown, stools hurled and a wave of people running from left to right, ducking and throwing punches. All that was needed now was a gun to be produced. Esquelita was well known for shootings so I could have been concerned, but not tonight – my favourite image was watching the stampede of macho blacks and Latinos, who moments earlier had been dancing, strutting and flexing, now running screaming for the coat check. The show was over, the coat-check queen fraught under a snowstorm of coat tickets. But what more could you want from Esquelita – a drag queen performance, a dramatic showdown and a full-on brawl. Sometimes all is well with the world.

•

Over the week I checked out a couple of other places when I was there on my spiritual visit. Recommended was a weekly event called Happy Endings, held in a Chinese massage parlour. Lounge in banquettes on the ground floor, or descend to the DJ-ready basement where the original steam rooms have been renovated as tiled booths. The name is a reference to the coy way in which the space's previous occupants used to offer clients a finale to their massage. Upon entering it seemed like any number of the bars you see, a fashionable, good-looking downtown crowd, mainly guys but a few girls too. Great mix. Then suddenly someone removed his clothes and mingled at the bar. The show had started. Next moment another naked man, bound and on a lead (wearing a chicken-head mask) was held down and wrapped up in gaffer tape until he was entirely restrained. Now if you are expecting more don't hold your breath because this was the performance. So New York. Everyone applauded. Well, I ask you. Talent? Glad it's not dead. The performance was actually a signal for the festivities to begin – the downstairs lounge was opened on the stroke of midnight and I ventured down. The room had walls of shower rooms in which sex displays were taking place (young men/older men/blow jobs). As everyone moved from upstairs the room became busy, the customers encouraged to participate in the tableaux, and well before you know it it's an orgy. A sleazefest – this is how New York used to be. I left the Romanesque scenes of debauchery satisfied that some things remain the same, and that can mean a great deal in these troubled times.

My final port of call was the Bijou, as it used to be called, but is now known as No. 82, situated on East 4th and 2nd. A jewel of a place and over the years a favourite. It was a porn cinema until recently when the rules changed and porn became forbidden. Let me explain: though it was technically a cinema, it was also a cruising and late-night sex venue, with rows of cubicles and corridors to explore. The cinema bit was just a front, but less of a front when it showed porn than what it shows now – regular Hollywood films. The patrons still cruise the lines of cubicles, often lodging themselves in for the entire evening, door ajar, attempting (mantis-like) to coax passers-by in for sex. And it's always the unattractive ones that hog the cubicles, everyone else padding round and round. Tonight the air was thick with grass smoke and the movie starred Mel Gibson; the irony was not lost on me that Mel was part of the soundtrack to a gay sex club. The grass fumes quickly made me feel heady and then nauseous. Enough was enough. I never really understood the appeal of grass and dope: laid out, barely able to function, munching endlessly on chocolate and pretzels, watching QVC because you can't find the remote.

I moved back into the cold night air. But I was glad to know that the Bijou was still there, still surviving, thriving, a sleazy side of New York: a sexual underground still servicing the horny New York night crawler. It did and still does fire my inspiration, fills me with hope that not all is sanitized in this new climate of moral and political change. So it seems I am not as jaded as I thought – New York still gives me a song or two.

•

It's been a long night and just before dawn I'm sat in a diner with my old friend Anita Sarko, declining her calamari rings, sipping tea and chatting about the passing years, and suddenly the past and present bump into each other. For sure, Anita had herself lived through hell and had emerged, luckily, unscathed though scarred. She looked terrific, long blonde tresses, glowing complexion and a doting younger husband. Neither of us are the scene stars we once were, but we had learnt from our hard-luck knocks to persevere and accept that less is the new more. God, a woman in New York learns the hard way or else ends up with two kids in Baltimore, an alcoholic husband she no longer knows and a life measured out in cups of coffee. Not Anita. She stuck it out and in the end was happy. She has a book planned, just as we all do, about her eventful life. The story of a girl from a rich Detroit family, rejected by her father, who went to law school, married, but threw it all away for a reckless dream. And she did. Succeed that is. She was the First Lady of the Turntables. She 'made it' in a world where women never had before. Anita has been influencing music and culture in New York City since 'Back in the Day'. She started at the Mudd Club, became the darling of the then unknown Beastie Boys, then went on to Danceteria, Area, Palladium and later at Serena, Lotus and Avalon!

She has spun everything, including parties for Prince, Jagger and Whitney; filled the ballroom floor at supermodel Natani's sweet-sixteen party; at the wedding of Sidney Lumet's daughter; and at Andy Warhol's funeral. We can still laugh, thank God, without being too maudlin. She hopes her dad will die one day and leave her a fortune, but she's not holding her breath. 'He never once helped me out, never once put his hand in his pocket, even at my lowest – and he'll outlive me I bet.' She laughs.

Anita *is* New York and, like the city itself you can't keep her down. Sat here now in the diner, with Anita picking at her food, we could have been back in the eighties: both blonde, with a little work here and there, trashing the same things, laughing over the same things. Everything had changed but somehow stayed intact.

I still hear songs, smells, sounds that ignite memories, I still feel free and youthful on its avenues and squares. I still love New York.

6

Barcelona

There is an old Catalan saying:
'Live today, work tomorrow, get your heart broken twice,
deny yourself nothing and die on a Monday'

•

Have you ever made an arrangement to meet up with an old lover? Someone with whom you once had a passionate affair, but time, routine and familiarity replace the passion then cuddles on the sofa watching a video supplant the sex, and you drift apart and it is over, though it was over long before you accept it?

Then years later comes the call out of the blue suggesting you get together, for a coffee, talk over old times, and reticently you agree and make an arrangement to meet up. Time itself has exorcized the demons, the jealousies, the memories of rows or the long silences; the gripes and sour grapes are long forgotten. So you don your rose-tinted spectacles, recall the good times, the laughs, the lust and choose to remember why you loved at all. What harm can it do? It's only a coffee after all. Absence makes the heart grow foolish. What will it be like meeting up after all these years? What if they've changed and for the better? That doesn't bode well. What if I've changed and for the worse? Will meeting up again destroy the good memories I still cherish? Would it be better to leave them intact? What about the passion – might it be rekindled? Do I want it to be: butterflies in the stomach, sticky palms and a racing pulse?

The love affair I'm referring to is not with a person at all but with a city: Barcelona.

What an affair we had.

•

I decided to return and meet up again after a fifteen-year hiatus. Our affair had been passionate and intense but over the years I felt betrayed by the change and progress I heard it had undergone. Barcelona was my secret place long before it was discovered by the hip and the wayward, before it was transformed into a tourist centre and commercial enterprise took hold, demolishing much of what I loved and cherished. So many places I had known were now closed down. I imagined it was to do with those damn Olympics – they sweep through city life like a Harpic rinse. I try not to be selfish, but I just can't help it. How can I change the habit of a lifetime? Barcelona shared by the world filled me with dread – not that I actually discovered it (though you'd think I did the way I'm going on). But I was there back in the early eighties before it was featured in every rough guide and trendy travel programme, normally with Magenta Devine loitering around every corner.

Nostalgia isn't what it used to be

•

But I felt that, despite all those programmes, they still left its dark side intact – in fact that was why it was loved by those of us in the know. Its bars, clubs, sleaze, its art and its flamboyant culture of mescaline-charged sangria-soaked late nights and early mornings. Barcelona noches. The Olympics could mean only one thing – clean-up time. I heard bars were closed, cabarets sanitized, sin-bin fleshpots fleeced and freshened up, by which I don't mean handy wipes and disinfectant. Sex shows could only be tolerated if no sex was involved (simulated or otherwise) and part nudity was the city order. Extra street lighting, new buildings, corporate food chains and tourist magnets would replace the seamier side of the city. More police patrols, zero tolerance, new malls, and a general lifting of the carpet to sweep the prostitutes and undesirables out of sight. Ruination as far as I was concerned. The Olympics were Barcelona's chance to show the world that it was a global player, and it certainly wasn't going to let a few bars, brothels, dealers or street prostitutes spoil that impression.

Most depressing for me was when I heard that Baños San Sebastian had been demolished to make way for luxury apartments. The San Sebastian outdoor pool built on the edge of the sea in the 1920s was an extraordinary and special place for me. I had used it as a backdrop in one of my videos (actually a toe-curling performance from me in which I leap from a tea chest delivering some speech about bitter oranges and . . . well anyway, it was all performance art stuff). At least I got it on film, the location that is. So many afternoons I would sunbathe there, listening to my fanstasico compilation tapes made for me by the NY drag performer Perfidia – all Latin and cha cha cha: the beautiful, crumbling, almost always deserted pool looking over the beach – it was all so *Suddenly, Last Summer*, and no guessing who I was.

On the horizon up the coast industrial works spilled out pollution into the sea and left trails of slime along the beach. When I first came I swam in the sea until I developed a fungal infection. Another time I had bathed naked, drifting, only to be disturbed by a group of fans standing over me taking photos and requesting autographs – oh, I could have died. Ah, such times. And I recall my best drug nights had been in Barcelona, the perfect place for the warm caress of ecstasy: the muted lights, the surrealism of the nightlife, the long neon techno nights, the charged sexuality of the clubs and the nights that never seemed to end. It's the simple things – a luxury hotel suite, money to waste and great drugs; now I ask you, it's not much to ask. What memories.

•

The last time I was here was for my friend Fran's birthday fifteen years ago and we all took ecstasy, hired a car and drove up to Tibidabo, a cathedral and fairground situated on the highest point overlooking the city. We visited the disco Martin's, and ended up relaxing at an infamous Barcelona sauna which doubled as a brothel; in the early hours we were the only people there relaxing by the pool. Memories are ghosts, you see, they whisper and chatter down the years, leaving imprints of who we are and what we did. Barcelona is full of ghosts; after all, it was the inspiration for a whole period in my creative life.

When I listen to the albums I made in that period, they can conjure up such memories. Back then in the mid-eighties when I looked just a little ridiculous with my sailor's hat perched atop my mohican haircut, leering out from the cover of *Sounds* magazine with the headline 'Filthy Marc!' I recall so much. I had accompanied a visiting journalist on a tour of the Barcelona flesh spots, which inevitably included a visit to an absinthe bar. I filmed the videos for 'Melancholy Rose' in Bar Marsella (on the corner of San Paul and San Roman) and 'Mother Fist' in the forgotten music hall La Paloma (Tigre 27). I've never seen anything like it. Red velvet banquettes in boxes around the dance floor, extravagantly painted ceiling, ornate plasterwork, and dazzling lights make it the dance hall of your dreams. I also filmed on the deck of a replica Spanish galleon forever dry-docked in the port at Barcelonetta. A young man called Ramon played the part of a sailor (as opposed to a hustler, a part he played every other night) and Nicky, a good friend, danced on the rooftop for the camera in the evening light, his face in white make-up as a lasting tribute (OK, I hate those Covent Garden mime artists – doesn't everyone?) to Lindsey Kemp. Lindsey Kemp is not a household name (except in the most depraved of households), but it is the name dropped by any young artiste wishing to invoke a bit of good old-fashioned decadence. Into the serious world of 1960s and 1970s British theatre, he injected a huge dose of camp, with productions drenched in blood and glitter, full of pansexual orgies and naked young men. He was now a resident of Barcelona and someone I regularly met taking tea in Plaza Real or propping up the bar at Kike.

I hear too the soundtrack of that time, can smell the sawdust, cheap perfumeries, the sea, paella, and of course the drains. For any of you who have been to Barcelona and walked around the Barrio Chino (the drunken sailor's pleasure quarter of Barcelona's sea port) or the Barrio Gótica area you will know what I mean. Barcelona is beautiful, but it stinks. The Kike Bar was situated down a back street from which piss was thrown from balconies upon noisy or unsuspecting people. It was a typical bar that inspired the Spanish artist and illustrator Nazario to create the character Anarcoma (a strapping transvestite supersleuth in the cartoon 'The Ghetto of Barcelona') who inspired me to write a tribute song of the same name.

I never met Nazario, fearing he would tell me he didn't like it. But part of me wishes I had met him. I found his number recently but could never call. I often wish I had the courage to meet the people I admire, but given the choice I always bottle out. If only I was good at mingling and parties and networking I'm sure my career would have benefited from it in some way – all that, oh darling, kiss kiss, oh you must do this charity gala I'm organizing, Marc, or, darling, you should sing on the film I'm doing ... They say that fortune favours the brave, so is there any wonder that I am such a pauper.

•

Having returned at last to Barcelona, I want to celebrate La Mercè festival, marking the end of summer. This is the festival for Barcelona's patron saint – Nostra Senyora de la Mercè – held in the week of 24 September, the day of La Mercè. This is a time of big celebrations with four days of musical performances, parades of giants and big-headed figures, fireworks, the impressive correfocs (fearsome creatures) that run through the streets of the city – dragons breathing fire, pagan rituals with devils, and exploding rockets. It seems that hell has disgorged itself into the streets of Barcelona.

Old habits die hard, so whenever I go to Barcelona I always stay in the same place: the Colon Hotel, 7 Avenida Catedral, in a room with a balcony that gives you front row seats for the festival procession below. Open the windows onto the balcony and you will understand what a room with a view really means. At dusk, the cathedral exquisitely lit, its Gothic spires circled by screaming swifts, really has to be experienced.

The view is everything because room service is virtually non-existent, the bathrooms nothing special, drunken revellers keep you from sleeping at night and elderly Spanish couples sing and dance on the square, waking you every morning. Having said that, the air conditioning is pretty good (when it's working) and the shutters keep out the light. But this time I noticed outside on the square below a stage had been erected upon which a Spanish singer was wailing and it was already just past midnight. This didn't bode well for a good night's sleep. But sleep? What am I thinking? This is Barcelona – the all-night city that doesn't even start until 2 or 3 a.m. at least. But my years of late-night clubbing are now ten years since, when we had cocaine, mescaline, ecstasy and alcohol. Now about all I have bothered to smuggle in is a box of camomile tea.

•

At first glance Barcelona appeared not to have changed at all. I noticed that even the hotel staff were the same, albeit older of course: they welcomed me back like an old friend (after a gap of fifteen years – now that's customer relations!) and I felt guilty I had deserted them for so long, especially when they offered me a choice of room (this was the peak season and the weekend of the pagan festival) with a ringside view from the balcony. The hotel decor looked the same, as did the carpet. I suddenly remembered all those years ago I had hidden tabs of acid under the carpet corner just behind a Moorish statue. I checked (out of curiosity) to see if they were still there, but no.

Looking through an old diary from 1986 I found this entry I'd made after one hot druggy night, and it shows what times I had.

Saturday 16 August 1986. These feelings won't go away. On my way in I thought how the hotel looked like a burnt silky peach dream encased in a marinated smoked tofu cube. The slat blinds, chiffon ruched drapes and heavy caramel curtains effectively snub out the sun that claws its way into the room. I can finally crawl between the cool white sheets, a film of drug sweat and sunblock-cream residue covering my skin like scum after a weird night out in the Spanish port . . .

You get the picture. These ramblings only go to illustrate that it was and still is, all reassuringly familiar. I was ready to fall in love all over again.

Having checked in successfully, the next thing is to take a stroll (not walk) down the Ramblas, and then into the narrow dark chasms of the Barrio Chino. The Ramblas is a long straight thoroughfare that runs from Plaza Cataluña down to the port, dividing the Barrio Chino and the Barrio Gótico. Down the centre of this road a wide pathway divides it, upon which stalls and booths sell magazines, live birds and animals, all manner of souvenir paraphernalia and flower arrangements. Between the stalls are outdoor cafes where you can sit and watch the parade pass by: local street performers, beggars, pedlars and musicians who vie for your attention and change. More often than not it is a fabulous freak show of brain-addled lunatics, which Barcelona seems so adapt at producing – singers (I use the term generously), dancers (even more generously), fortune tellers (always toothless), performing dogs or cats or anything that can turn a trick, fakirs, magicians, monocyclists, soothsayers, mystics, and some performances that are so pointless and inept they are quite cutting edge – in Britain they would get a grant and a short season at the ICA. Then there are the mime artists – mime, clowns and ballet, uhm? Mime and especially those really annoying living statues – what the hell are they about? Standing still, now that's a talent.

So I sat in Cafe de l'Opera, one of the most famous and elegant cafes on the side of the Ramblas, and sipped my Horchetta (nectar of the gods, a Spanish drink, though Egyptian originally, made from chufa nuts, and it's just so delicious even trendy Manhattan delis now sell it) and tried my utmost to ignore the pleading hoards of beggars, hoping they would leave me in peace. The Ramblas on a warm summer evening is incomparable. The closer you get to the harbour the sleazier it becomes, until, near the bottom, the roads that lead into the Barrio Chino are alive with transvestite bars, topless go-go bars, and some of the roughest-looking whores ever seen in any European port (sagging breasts, moustaches and corned beef legs). They stand around touting, shouting, intimidating and threatening, so caked in garish make-up it is difficult to tell the real women from the transsexuals (often Brazilians saving up enough for their chop-chop cheap op back home in Rio).

I was happy to discover that since my last visit nothing much had really changed, or if it had then it had soon enough changed back. Only the port at the bottom of the Ramblas has vastly altered, commercially changed beyond recognition. The little fish restaurants were gone, torn down to make way for the Olympic village. The Barrios San Sebastian and Barcelonetta too have changed forever. A single restaurant complex now dominates a fake marina surrounded by luxury developments. I thought it would sadden me but it actually seemed an improvement on my old memories: of course I miss sitting on the beach at my favourite little restaurant eating paella and staring out to sea. God, I sound like Shirley Valentine – pull yourself together.

I ventured off the Ramblas into one of the many dark side alleys of San Paul. Once this road had a reputation as violent. It was where I got attacked by a knife-wielding drug dealer while I was trying to buy hashish; I actually managed to climb into a taxi as the man leapt on me, screaming hysterically as we drove away. I'd upset him by reneging on a deal when buying his hash, due to the fact that I suspected it was actually a meat stock cube. Bad move.

So here I was again, back walking down the same street, its narrowness allowing the houses to almost touch several floors up. The street is San Ramon, perhaps the worst of all the streets here, populated then and now with African drug dealers, pimps and generally not the type of people you would want to share a syringe with, or even a sweet sherry. Now it didn't seem quite as threatening as a decade earlier. Maybe it was something to do with the strategically built new police station nearby.

In Barcelona's Barrio Chino – the infamous warren of narrow streets where Jean Genet set *A Thief's Journal* – I returned to Bar Marsella, still intact as a kind of monument to the fast-fading bohemia of the Barrio Chino. It is the place where years earlier I drank absinthe (La Fe Verte), the nine-teenth-century hallucinogen that, in its time, had ruined more lives than cocaine. I watched people prepare glasses at their tables – dissolving sugar, flame and water turn the absinthe milky green, the colour Oscar Wilde described as opaline. I no longer drink it, having left that poison behind, and have no doubts that it is poison. In Russia, the plant is ominously called *chernobyl*; even absinthe's Greek name, *apsinthion*, means 'undrinkable'. I recall Oscar Wilde's description of absinthe's effects: 'After the first glass, you see things as you wish they were. After the second glass, you see things as they are not. Finally you see things as they really are, and that is the most horrible thing in the world.'

But though the bar looked the same, still nicotine-stained, the ceilings an autumnal gold, and the mirrors and bottles coated in a thick layer of dust, the old locals had gone, replaced by a young trendier crowd. But at least it was preserved intact, and still there.

•

There was one place I needed to return to: the Bagdad Club
– the sex cabaret club that featured as part of its entertainment (quite marvellously documented in my autobiography)
a dwarf sex act, a black on white act (a well-endowed black
man . . .), a mechanical horse act complete with rider who
sits on a saddle and dildo, transsexual lesbian acts, and a
hermaphrodite spider-fly sex act. Basically not your average
family fare. Between each sexual delectation was a Spanish
compère-cum-comedian who told jokes and made lewd ref-
erences to the size of audience members' members. Finally,
as a climax to the evening, a magician performed dove
and card tricks while a strong man pulled members of
the audience across the stage via a chain, hook and penis
piercing. Well, you just have to take my word for it.

So I was looking forward to seeing how much the acts
had developed their, uhm, acts. Firstly, and to my relief, it
still looked the same: a sort of Moroccan restaurant covered
in mosaic and a little stage which featured the revolving
bed on which the spectaculars took place. But things had
changed. This time we were treated to a show of old Spanish pornographic cartoons set to an overloud soundtrack.
When the show did eventually begin they were no more
than a procession of lesbian bondage acts, which seemed to
neither delight nor stimulate the audience who sat blankly
staring.

Gone were all the freaks of old, and soon enough so was
I. I know what you're all thinking, the world has moved on,
the freak show is no more, we've all accepted that the world
has changed. Well, not me. I like nothing more than an
old-fashioned pay and gawp freak show, and you know
what, I don't think any of us has the right to take away a
freak's right to work in the name of political correctness.
And the other contentious issue for me was that the Bagdad

charged me around £50 to see what I can get for free on MTV in a Tatu video.

•

Walking back towards the Ramblas, I checked out some of my favourite little bars. Most of the transvestite bars have long since gone, but among all the boarded-up sites still stands Bar La Concha, now a shrine to the Spanish icon and film actress Sara Montiel. Every inch of the tiny bar, from floor to ceiling, is decorated with pictures, portraits, paintings, posters and film stills of Miss Montiel. Resembling a cross between Dietrich and Hayward, vamp and gypsy, she looks down from a vast array of likenesses through her golden heyday to her cameo and cabaret years, surrounded in the bar every night by adoring gay men, something one suspects she would have loved. Now she is the patron saint of Concha, bathed in red light and candle shine, the guardian angel of the Moroccan rent boys who sit at the bar and chat with elderly sponsors who may assist them at worst with their next meal, at best through English college.

Around the corner is another favourite little bar. Bar Pastís (Santa Mónica Street) is located in the centre of Barcelona, next to the Ramblas, and is one of the most well-known and visited bars of the city. French music, bohemian atmosphere and rustic decoration are its main signs of identity. Packed with paintings, dusty bottles, burnt-down candles – the sort of back-street bar where Picasso would have doodled on the napkins and Dali sipped pastis with a kohl-eyed Gala, the flavour flamenco and revolution and dreams of bad poetry.

I was satisfied the Barrio Chino had, despite my ten years' absence, retained much of its charm, just as I had remembered it.

I flicked through my free guide, which I had picked up at a sex shop behind Plaza Real, called Sextienda. It is rather a dubious sort of place with an extensive video selection (most featuring rather, uhm, youthful participants). It also has three or four cabins where one can, should one be so inclined, find companionship for a few minutes. This is entirely hearsay, you understand, having never ventured further than the art books and erotic ceramics section.

I had decided, for the purpose of research, of course, to visit one of Barcelona's many gay brothels. For the sake of discretion we shall call it Caesar's; though not its actual name, it is close enough for anyone interested to find it in the guide. Not coincidentally it is decorated in a Roman style, with fake columns and of course a statue of David. Classy. It is situated near Thermos sauna, a world-famous (if you're in the know) establishment of ill repute.

I eventually found the brothel, which was no more than a private apartment. The door was cautiously opened by an unshaven, slightly rotund young man in a linen suit, badly creased, and sporting sandals. He beckoned me inside, virtually kowtowing as I entered. This general toadying I took to mean one of two things – business was bad and he was overjoyed to have a visitor, or he had recognized me.

Sometimes I forget I'm me and that I'm, if not famous, recognizable. I feel a little uneasy when visiting such places; I am conscious of mirrors possibly concealing hidden cameras. It never bothered me until one time when I was invited, for research purposes, to a similar establishment in Earls Court where I was shown by one of the young men (the proprietor was away) to a central room. This looked outward to all the adjacent rooms via two-way mirrors while clients indulged their every whim with the hustlers. Now I always wonder who is behind every mirror; perhaps some

News of the World reporter with a video camera and sordid headline: Surprise! Not that I imagine I'm that newsworthy but one never knows if one is being set up for something.

So I felt a little nervous, checking out the mirrors and looking for a suitable escape route. I was shown a chair in the centre of the room as the rotund young man excused himself. Looking round it was all very Wildean: velvet wallpaper, ruched drapes, thoughtfully furnished, quite tasteful – an establishment of quality. The man returned and I was shown the bedrooms, each decorated individually in a sort of brothel chic: plush bedding, low red lighting (very flattering, which is a good thing), drapes, fake furs (a nightmare to get stains out of). The overall impression was comfortable, twee and kind of erotic. But each one had a mirror, those floor to ceiling ones that made me feel particularly uneasy. The bedside table was replete with condoms, lubricant, towels and tissues. A TV in the corner was showing porn (strikes me that if you need porn you shouldn't be here). All came en suite. He explained that a shower must be taken before . . . whatever. I was shown back to the reception room and took a seat. Then the door opened and a line of young men stood before me for my inspection, marched in from some antechamber in the back of the flat. A motley selection as ever I saw, the less attractive ones trying to muster a smile or flirt, the rest unable to contain their utter boredom, jaded and sulky; every bit of enthusiasm had been drained out of them, so to speak.

I then made my apologies and left. Oh yes I did. I was tempted though, by the least attractive one, who tried all he could to get me to pick him and, short of swinging from the chandeliers and pulling every pick-me expression known to man, gave his utmost. But I wasn't going to be the first to pick him, though I must say enthusiasm is nine-tenths of the attraction. On the way out the host apologized while virtually prostrating himself at my feet, eventually offering himself at a much reduced rate. But, as the stinking hobo said to Claudia Schiffer, 'Sorry, love, you're just not my type.' I'm sure he'll give the young men a hard time later. None of them seemed to be there by force and all seemed well over the age of consent, so I didn't dwell on the moral aspect.

I was glad to be outside in the afternoon sunshine, instead of in that oppressive brothel, which made me feel deflated. What a joyless experience Caesar's had turned out to be. Now I'm not going to discuss the merits of prostitution but providing people do it by consent and are old enough then so be it. In honesty I felt guilty, particularly for rejecting them – not that I suspect they dwelt on it for a minute – but because I know what it is like to be rejected. Twenty years ago I would have probably picked them all, but it seemed with middle age I had become quite prudish. I was trying to retrace my steps but was now seeing things differently. I hadn't wanted the world to change but was discovering it actually hadn't, only that I had.

·

Perhaps Thermos, the brothel disguised as a sauna, would be more revealing, so in I popped. After all, I was passing.

What I like about Thermos is, apart from anything else, it is just a great place to hang out and just watch what is going on. And what is going on is prostitution: no one goes there for the sauna (I don't even know if it actually has one). The place is full most of the time with young Spanish and Moroccan men who virtually live there, and offer their services to anyone interested. Laid out over several floors there are cabins, a cinema, restaurant, jacuzzi and rather murky pool. Early evenings are the busiest as young men look to make money for the night ahead.

Swarthy hustlers sat in the half light of the cabins smoking

joints and trying to attract my attention as I passed, waving
often larger than average cocks in my direction. The soundtrack was eighties music; in fact it always is. Occasionally
I hear one of my songs and lurk in the darkness until it
finishes. Red walls, smoke, half-naked guys wrapped in
towels, the sound of flip-flops flip-flopping down corridors
and in the gloom tropical fish swim in algae-stained tanks
wondering what the hell happened to the sunlight, a perfect
analogy for the hustlers who circle endlessly round. After half
an hour word seemed to get round that I was not interested
in business and then I became invisible. Staff traipsed round
intermittently checking the cabins, collecting soggy towels
and spraying down the plastic mattresses before wiping them.
On the floor were strewn used condoms and empty popper
bottles, discarded by the spent. Downstairs in the restaurant
hustlers ate meals, their constitutions able to deal with the
dubious-looking food that minutes earlier had cockroaches
scampering over it. I noticed in the cold cabinet an avocado
and prawn salad covered in a glutinous Marie Rose sauce, a
cockroach struggling for its life embedded in the sticky substance. The chef noticed and picked out the insect, flicking it
to the floor.

When Thermos was emptying out in the early hours I sat
on one of the plastic garden chairs by the pool and listened:
in the quiet my memories of the years came back in sounds
of laughter and good times. Those late nights and early
mornings seemed instilled into the place. Thermos is the best
for this. So many memories, those ghosts again, dormant for
so long, now awake and whispering stories of those carefree
times. They are tinged now with sadness for what was and
will not be again. I hear them more and more as I retread
the past.

·

Back outside, I simply walked. So much has changed about Barcelona. In my absence I need not have worried for the city has blossomed into one of the most beautiful places in the world, where old and modern sit side by side, daringly upstaging each other. Yet the old port sleaziness and the fashionable new caress each other. Barcelona was and remains so utterly stylish, paradoxically reinvented and traditional, an open secret, a public hermit. Obsessed with playful and radical interpretations of everything from painting to theatre to urban design and development, Barcelona consistently surprises in its constant quest for emotion and self-renewal.

Sitting on the balcony of my room at the Colon Hotel at midnight, I watched the parade under the window, literally a parade of people dancing, singing, lighting fireworks and roman candles, bearing staffs of sparks that waterfall on the cobbles, dodging the great fire-breathing dragons: this is a pagan celebration that has been repeated over the centuries and breathes life into tradition.

I was lucky to be here and to have Barcelona back in my life. It hadn't let me down. We've matured together and like old lovers we've found a common ground from the closeness of our intimate past. And we can drink and laugh in each other's company again. Who knows? Next a passionate kiss and then . . .?

•

I left Barcelona knowing that I would regularly return again, and it is one place that I now know I could happily end my days. I looked up at the departures board and saw my flight to Paris was on last call. I moved towards the gate.

7

Paris

'Avec des "si" on mettrait Paris en bouteille'
(With 'if's' one could put Paris in a bottle)

•

Paris was another old lover of mine. It indulged all my Genet fantasises, and let me pretend to be Brel and Greco's secret son.

In short, I could be as self-indulgent and pretentious as hell, and it never questioned me. Being pretentious in Paris makes entire sense. It is a place to be the sensualist, to be existential, sexually aloof, a place to talk utter tosh.

It never took anything from me and let me reinvent myself however I desired. Over the years our relationship has lasted the course.

Paris is the ultimate showpiece, a city of staggering beauty, awesome design and architecture, a living work of art, a flirt and a terrible snob, and quite unlike anywhere else in the world. Paris has meant so much to me, especially through its literature and its music, none more so than Chanson. French Chanson, like ripe camembert, does not travel well. Artists and songs that are known and revered all over the French-speaking world are completely unknown almost anywhere else, and certainly if known at all it is not for their sustained repertoire. Chanson was a direct development from a cabaret tradition that had produced Edith

Piaf, Maurice Chevalier and Charles Trenet. Where the new generation of singers differed was in their message. Aznavour sang about homosexuality and genocide. Léo Ferré, a household name in France, sang about atheism, paedophilia and bereavement. Barbara, the most dramatic diva of French chanson, is famous for songs about loneliness, Aids and seducing men half her age. Chanson has thus been a major influence in my creative life, and I have come to love so much about it. I have often thought about living in Paris, but I suppose I'm afraid to commit, afraid that I might grow complacent and over time lose all I love about it under the daily routine of being there.

Paris is the beautiful jewel in France's crown, unashamedly snobbish and outrageously rude. I love to book myself into the red-velvet-lined Oscar Wilde room at L'Hôtel (the room where he actually died, the shock of the bill adding to his final demise), or the silver Mistingette room at the same hotel (L'Hôtel is situated on the Rue de Beaux Arts on the Left Bank) – Jim Morrison stayed there when in Paris, Mick Jagger counts it amongst his favourites. An oasis for the bohemian, a hidden treasure. At one time I stayed there week in, week out until I decided I couldn't afford its 'special room' and moved to a more affordable one (meaning a pokey velvet-lined cupboard), with barely room to turn around in the bathroom, but still it seemed more luxurious than far grander hotels I've stayed in. You can even book the indoor pool for one private hour. As you enter the lobby from a quiet residential side street and look straight up at the cupola running six floors up to an ornate skylight, you will be amazed. Its modest facade belies its flamboyant interiors. It is an extravaganza you could only find in Paris, a heady mixture of art and whimsy! L'Hôtel is as entertaining as Paris itself.

When L'Hôtel is full, I stay at Hôtel Meurice (228 Rue de Rivoli). This venerable hotel, whose present location dates from 1835, has been restored to its former opulence. The grey and cream marble floored reception area is flanked by seven-foot-tall Italian white-marble candelabra swagged with gilt garlands. It has an old-style opulence and is surpisingly cheaper than L'Hôtel (maybe that isn't that surprising, but it is especially cheap in August). The rooms are grand but frayed, the wardrobes smell of mothballs and money, and haughty old women bundle toy dogs under their arms whilst taking tea.

My final choice, and clearly this is not a backpacker's guide, is the Hôtel Costes (which should be called 'Costal-otta'), located between the Place Vendôme and, naturally, the Louvre. The ground floor has been turned into a romantic maze of tables, so customers constantly wend their way past everyone else.

The Costes is so painfully hip that it is in danger of imploding on itself: I remember on my first visit, before even reaching the reception desk, I bumped into Bjork and Sharleen Spiteri. The music being played throughout the lobby is even available on a Costes soundtrack CD at reception – a sure sign of trendiness. So there are three recommendations, all over-priced, with bad service and terrible attitude – but that's Paris.

•

I have to confess that there were two reasons I had to visit Paris, other than having no reason which is usual, and they were to film a video for a forthcoming single due for release, and perform a short set at a party.

Piece of cake.

First the video – what a palaver that was. The director had an idea which featured me squeezed into a Gaultier corset adorned with feathers, my face encrusted with thousands of diamonds and sequins – three hours to apply, followed by eight hours standing around and a further two hours to hours to

Hanging out in Soho circa 1983.

With the undisputed queen of burlesque, the ravishing Dita Von Teese.

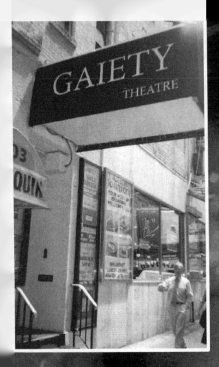

Top left: The Gaiety, New York – still hanging on in there. Top right: Performance art – Baby Doll tribute piece – so New York. Bottom left: One of New York's greatest bars – gone forever.
Bottom right: It must be Thanksgiving because someone's hiding the turkey – San Francisco, 2002.

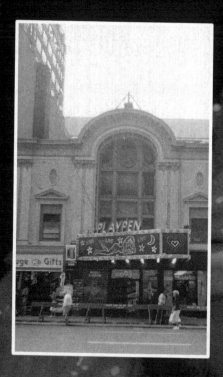

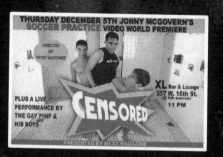

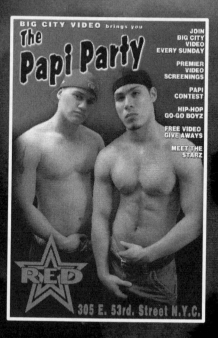

Assorted images of lost New York.

Top: The infamous Bagdad club in Barcelona, once a freak show, now only showing pseudo-lesbian shenanigans. Above left: Barcelona Cathedral from my hotel room. Above right: Bar Marsella. The absinthe bar is amazingly still here.

Opposite: Barcelona *noches*. Photos: © Neil X.

CITY VARIETIES
MUSIC HALL

Harry London, Charlie Chaplin and
vaudeos performed in this Music
Hall built in 80's for Charles
Thornton on the site of the
White Swan coaching Inn

famous venue of the
"Good Old Days"
first broadcast
in 1953

CITY VARIETIES
MUSIC HALL

The Flanagan and Allen Story
A New Musical
Thursday 20th May 7.30pm

Chris Barrie & Norman Lovett
A fantastic double bill of stand up comedy

MARC ALMOND

Saturday 22 May 8.00pm

The Eleanor Rigby Experience
A Unique Interpretation of the Works of
Lennon & McCartney

Jimmy Tarbuck
With Special Guest Kenny Lynch
Thursday 27th May 7.30pm

Following the George Michael trail, LA, 2002.

Are you the only one who's turned up for my CD signing?

Top left: A familiar club name, a different town. Top right: Come into my pleasure palace, Hamb

remove the mask. What was that about, I thought. The director, noting my concern, assured me that after post-production edit it would look 'magnifique!' They would erase my legs from the shot and create the effect of my torso attached to a dress-dummy stand against a backdrop of a music box. Don't ask the significance. It's just very surreal and glamorous (I'm assured) and so very French. The filming was as they always are, a long-drawn-out affair involving numerous flamboyant make-up artists, stylists, and costumiers mincing around and turning any minor crisis into a major drama.

Eventually back in my hotel I had to get myself ready to do a guest performance at a hip Parisian party (this was the second reason for my visit). Knowing what Parisian parties are like I began to regret being talked into doing it, but ever the professional I set off. All my fears were justified – as per normal in Paris everyone was so busy being fabulous and taking copious amounts of drugs that the little things like organizing a stage, sound system and lights had been entirely overlooked. I eventually ended up performing in a corner at floor level, into a microphone that kept cutting out or feeding back. I just went along with it. Everyone was so fucked up and caught up their own gorgeousness that no one complained, dancing and singing along (those that weren't entirely oblivious of me and chatting away). So why put myself through it, you may ask. Because I just can't resist that lure of something hip, it might just rub off.

•

Part of the Paris that I love is its cultural mix of French and Arabic, rich and exotic. The history of colonialism is now an integral part of the city, adding to the hues and tones of its culture. And one senses that Paris changes very slowly, the past is its present, and life is celebrated in its uniqueness. No other place goes to such lengths to protect its culture like

Paris, and the French steadfastly refuse to embrace globalism. They have their own music, art, films, food, architecture, attitude – and as such a clearly defined national identity.

Visiting some of my favourite places I was both delighted and disappointed. The Folies Bergère has become aware of its own kitsch, and panders too much to its now mainly gay audience. The Moulin Rouge has also changed since Baz Luhrmann made the film, parodying itself. But thankfully I found the Crazy Horse club still relatively unchanged. The most beautiful girls cavort across the most fabulous of settings, still a triumph of style and design over content, though the interpretive dance, puppet show and conjuror left me a bit bemused.

Later that evening I strolled down Rue Blondel, a street famous for its 'affordable' prostitutes, women well past their prime, dressed in gaudy transparent outfits leaning against walls, and the occasional one (I kid you not) in a split skirt and beret. Paris is its own living cliché. The street is a show, a cabaret of life. The Rue Blondel, Rue St Denis Bans and all their various sex establishments, set pieces against which prostitutes strut and pose whilst swarthy men smoke Galoises in half-lit doorways. It is so perfect that all the men need are striped shirts, to pick their teeth with flick knives and spit on the ground while an accordion plays from a distant cafe to complete the scene. The very Hollywood Piafness of it all, Irma La Douce and Shirley MacLean. I almost expect one of the swarthy guys to grab a prostitute by her black tresses for an Apache dance. Forget the Crazy Horse or the Folies Ber-gère (the ticket prices are exorbitant anyway), here on certain streets in Paris is a free show, twice nightly. I noticed a young man follow a prostitute through a small door and imagined her leading him up some crooked stairs to a garret room that overlooks the Paris rooftops to Notre-Dame. Taking her in his arms, he caresses her neck with kisses whilst she drains the glass of red wine and wipes her mouth with the back of her hand. Bill Bryson couldn't have put it better.

I strolled on, past manicured parks where old men play boules, anaemic women weighed down in opulent furs are pulled along by ridiculous poodles, and lovers clinch in shadowy doorways.

Onwards past swish restaurants decorated as peasant rococo, and appealing apartments where pools of warm light give tantalizing glimpses of walls lined with books, pencil sketches and decorative antiques. I love to walk around and look into other people's houses – it's a getting older sort of pastime, noting the decor or deriding the lack of taste. But Paris apartments seem so inviting, so tasteful and say to the tourist passing by: how lucky we are to live in such a place, and be able to gaze out across such a wondrous city.

I made an unhurried circuit of Notre-Dame and leaned over a railing by the Seine to watch the boats float by, trimmed with tiny lights, lost adrift in the hopeless romance of it all. Paris is the place to gather your thoughts, to relive the past and re-evaluate.

As I searched for something, answers begin to come to me. The French, for all their faults, seem to understand something of what life is about, and it has mostly to do with living. Surround yourself with beauty, take time to make time for sensual pleasures, and life will reward you. Paris is about quality. Real coffee takes patience and love to make properly, there are no short cuts – don't deprive yourself of the effort it takes because that is part of the reward.

I dined in a half-empty restaurant on a side street in the magical Marais district. Personally I am not a fan of French food: too many rich sauces for me, all presentation and not much substance. But it was served impeccably with just the right side order of disdain. The dessert was unpronounceable (on the English menu it is explained that the description is beyond translation) but it turned out to be no more than a crème caramel infused with brandy.

Paris has an engagingly private-club atmosphere, which not only emphasizes your exclusion but positively celebrates it. Even the French who live outside of Paris complain of this. Parisians are renowned for their rudeness. Once they hear a foreign accent or French rural dialect they react like you are infectious. Taxi drivers are the worst culprits, that's if you can ever encounter one in the first place. Getting a taxi in Paris is near impossible. You can't just flag one, oh no, that would be far too logical a solution. You must find one of the several taxi ranks situated secretly around the city, and then it must be 'in use' (not all ranks work twenty-four hours), then having found one you must take your place in a long queue and wait. And wait. And wait.

Still, not getting a taxi gives you an excuse to walk and a chance to discover a side of the real Paris.

•

Back at my hotel, preparing to go out for the night, I asked the hotel clerk to call me a taxi. He looked at me with contempt and disgust. 'Oh, I don't think that will be possible.'

He then returned to reading his ledger.

Oh, all right then, I thought to myself, maybe I'll just go back to my room for the night.

I resignedly stormed out into the night, a couple of addresses scribbled on bits of paper. Quite how the Germans put up with the French attitude for four years of occupation is quite a feat if you ask me.

A little earlier my publisher had called up enquiring how everything was going and suggesting it might be a good idea, being in Paris and all, to take the opportunity to visit a few 'of those unusual' places the readers would love to hear about, for inclusion in the book. Of course it wasn't said as plainly as that but I clearly understood what was meant.

So here goes.

The first place I visited was a club called L'Arène (80 Quai de l'Hôtel de Ville), situated near Porte de Lilles on the bank of the Seine. It is an indistinguishable place, which upon entering seems an intimate bar but quickly becomes apparent that it is a sex club. Three floors of cabins, dark rooms and shadowy corners. The clientele are generally attractive, which I discovered doesn't bode well because they are picky and spend the entire time waiting for someone they feel is worthy of their attention. They'll probably end up going home with the one person who finally lives up to their unrealistic expectations, themselves. Parisians are undoubtedly some of the most attractive people you would hope to find, but their arrogance and bad attitude can be intimidating. And their bad breath (which I know might sound like a generalization) is always a real obstacle. Even the most angelic of them need a few tips in dental hygiene – take my word for it.

I left and headed towards another club called the Depot (10 Rue aux Ours). I was sure that this was the place to go, a Parisian pleasure palace unrivalled. Naturally my expectations were high. I eventually arrived after being lost down several back streets, walking for almost an hour, and staving off several threatening encounters with Middle Eastern types. Mind you, it is hard to take any threat seriously when spoken in French.

When I arrived I discovered a huge queue outside the club and, though tempted to leave, took my place at the end. Then I noticed every so often people would approach the front of the queue, push in or duck under the barrier past people, ignoring the queue. The French are remarkably shameless about this, and no one protested which surprised me; for a nation that takes pride in its rudeness this seemed like a missed opportunity. But despite myself, I am just too British to jump a queue.

Eventually I was inside what is a cavernous disco. At first confused as to why it was so empty having seen so many people barge their way in, I realized that everyone was downstairs. I descended the steep stairway into a vast labyrinth of walkways, rooms, cabins and corridors that seemed to twist and turn endlessly. Lining the walls men stood cruising, eyeing each other up and down before joining the moving throng – an endless treadmill of unrealized possibilities. Unlike L'Arène, where there were just a few people, here there were just too many. Choosing the wrong person for a quick liaison could mean missing a better one.

I thought of the deeply profound lyrics of the Sinitta song:

> So many men, So little time,
> How can I choose?

I began to suspect that no one was ready to make a commitment of five minutes until all options had been weighed up. And in such a highly competitive marketplace, I was in danger of being entirely overlooked.

I have a French friend, a fashion designer, who informed me that he had many sexual encounters at the Depot, because, as he modestly put it, 'I am simply the most beautiful person there.' After hearing this, and after picking my jaw up off the floor, I had to admire his arrogance and irony-free self-belief. That is so French, I thought, an English person could never say that.

I wandered through the maze of possibilities, past small rooms, past men lounging on banquettes (how perfectly named), past cabins where men eyed you up and gestured for you to not even think about entering unless you were the offspring of Alain Delon. Again it was simply about finding someone for anonymous sex, as it was in every gay sex club in every city across the world. It began to unsettle me. The idea of anonymous sex is far sexier than the reality. It goes back to my original thoughts about eroticism. Here there was no communication of self, no anticipation, no eroticism – just a meat rack. High quality cuts of beef, may I add, well-hung game, but maybe a little past their sell-by dates and tough. Tenderizing was what most of them needed.

Personally I like to cruise, but I like the foreplay, court-ship, a casual brush, a sexual rapport, an appetizer, not straight to the main course with no possibility of a dessert or those little pink mint bonbons. This place was a banquet but it seemed everyone was starving.

As the evening wore on I could see the alcohol take hold of many, and an air of desperation descended. People pushed and shoved as though at the opening of the Harvey Nichols sale, clambering for last season's reductions. As the place emptied out, those who had ignored me earlier began to cruise me, lowering their standards as they watched their options deplete.

By now the place was sweltering, the smell of amyl nitrate and spent possibilities infusing the air. I sat at the bar watching the parade trundle by, looking more and more frantic. I thought it better to sit and wait, hoping that all good things come eventually. Suddenly a youngish man, not unattractive, sat next to me, giving me the once-over. He edged his stool closer, and then tantalizingly reached into his bulging pocket and pulled out a pair of surgical rubber gloves, stretching them and letting them snap back. He then nodded in the direction of the back room, indicating I should follow. Was this what it had come to? The only offer on the table was to give an internal examination? I politely declined. He seemed put out by my response. Slipping the gloves back into his pocket he edged closer. Introductions followed and, though French, he spoke good English. 'Maybe,' he said, 'you prefer if I let you use the gloves on me?'

I declined this offer. But I had to admire him, he wasn't asking anyone to do anything he wasn't willing to do himself. How romantic, I thought.

He gave me his phone number and suggested we could meet up, just for a coffee. I thanked him. He then told me he normally went to another club which was much heavier, meaning, I suppose, more extreme. I chose not to imagine what went on there. Maybe if I had been in New York, and maybe ten years earlier, I might have gone along for the ride, but in Paris now I wanted something more – more aesthetic, more meaningful, I suppose. I wanted Paris to fulfil me in other ways. I'm past all that. I want my Paris to be Greco, Piaf, Josephine Baker, Mistinguette, Aznavour. To be Mont-martre, Pigalle, accordions, red velvet drapes, strip clubs with exotic names like Narcisse, Genet, wide boulevards, the Christmas lights that line the Champs Elysées, the outdoor cafes, the Seine, Oscar Wilde in exile, Claude Françoise, Serge Gainsbourg and of course Dalida. I want to sit on that swing high above a stage against a faux Parisian backdrop depicting an Eiffel Tower outlined in twinkling lights. I suppose what I want from Paris are the clichés. That's what Paris is and gives. Almost a song. It wants to make me sing again, it restores romance.

As I made my excuses (am I always making excuses?) to my new friend at the bar, he made one last attempt to coax me:

'I have a butt plug in my ass right now. I never go out without it.'

Whatever reaction he was hoping for, I think he got.

'Oh, really,' I blurted out.

He smiled a Princess Diana coy flirty smile.

I swear he almost blushed. Maybe not.

8

Back to My Roots

'A young guy came up to me and he said, "Can I have your autograph? I want to follow in your footsteps." I told him, you better get yourself some comfortable shoes then.'

•

There are constant signs that tell me I'm feeling middle-aged. For example, I find myself buying CD compilations, more often than not those artists that I liked in my teens. Time has become precious and I just want everything encapsulated and tied up in a neat little bow. I've no time to listen to those dull self-indulgent album tracks, just the best bits – compilations neatly compartmentalizing entire careers into the sound-bite package.

Watching the News Channel is another sign of getting old. I could watch it 24/7, the same reports over and over again, hoping to glean some new fact about the world, fretting over it, feeling responsible, or omnipotent, feeling the weight of the world on my shoulders, and angry, just usually feeling *angry* about it all, whatever it might be.

Getting older means finding myself getting more and more intolerant and impatient. What happened to the laid-back liberal of old, I ask myself, fingering my love beads and measuring out the patchouli oil? That's a good question. Search me. He got cynical about the world.

I sit with all the other armchair politicians and shout at

the TV. Maybe I exaggerate but as I've grown older my view of the world has become a lot less rose-tinted. I don't think I'm a true cynic though. I'm much too romantically inclined. I take to heart that old cliché that 'there are none so blind', and that other old faithful, 'If you stand for nothing, you'll fall for anything' – in fact, just add your favourite cliché and apply liberally. I find myself welling up at patriotic songs and feel a stir of pride when I see 'our boys' in action (well, some kind of stirring occurs anyway). I view the moaners, wobblers, doubters and lily-livered liberals with caution at best, or stupid, misinformed and naive at worst. I feel I'm right because . . . well, I just damn know I am.

I feel in touch with the world through the news, and the world touches me.

I remember as a teenager how much I used to hate the news; it was that boring TV void that came after *Captain Pugwash* or *Magic Roundabout*.

As you get older, the news, seeing what is going on in the world, trying to make sense of it, I suppose, and getting your confused personality in some kind of order, become important. The first half of your life is for learning lessons, the second half for lying on the sofa, watching TV and generally acting disgruntled. Well, that's the theory anyhow.

I playback in my mind those old home movies: blowing out birthday candles aged eight, cautiously playing in rock pools and holding up a crab by its back leg for the camera, splashing around in the tide, and being wrapped in enormous soft towels, fragrant and line dried. These thoughts make me tearful and nostalgic. An old song on the radio, a dog-eared photo, a view, and of course a smell can reduce me to tears. How strange it is that smells, and the memory of them, evoke our strongest recollections, recall to us a precise moment or feeling or place: Playdough, school corridors, spent fireworks, charity shops, Copydex glue, leather upholstery, candyfloss, creosote, disinfectant, laundry detergent and fresh-cut grass. Childhood memories represent times when we were free from responsibilities, so we may redefine them in an idealized way, even though many of the experiences we went through were difficult.

Rooting through old treasure boxes and scrapbooks filled with photos of loves long past, of affectionate letters and scrawled memories, I find I can now read them or gaze upon them with a kind of pride, tell myself, 'Well, I didn't do so badly after all – I could pull them in my younger days.'

Then I find myself imagining my future days, in a Southport home for the prematurely senile (not too many years from now actually), and I'm surrounding myself with these trophies, pawing over the photos whilst listening to my old recordings (the depressing ones naturally), hair dye running down my overstretched and heavily powdered face whilst a sadistic nurse impatiently spoons mushed carrot and swede into my toothless mouth (the gold teeth long since pawned).

'Come on, Mr Almond, if you don't finish it you can't have the treacle sponge, and I'll have to confiscate your scrapbook.'

'No, nurse, no! Not my scrapbook, it's all I've left.' Then I tell her, 'They loved me, they really did.'

'Of course they did, now open wide,' she says, spooning more carrot mash in.

'I was famous once. I sold millions of records. I met Andy Warhol and Elton John.'

'If you say so, Mr Almond. Now Nurse Giles will bring your pudding and then I'll come back and give you a colonic, and if you don't complain you can watch the *Coronation Street* special eightieth anniversary.'

Old age seems a grim prospect, and I really can't think of anything good about it. Midlife is the home run, and it seems whatever way you look at it, it's a depressing prospect. I suppose there is always the chance that I might get a second shot at 'proper fame', like Tony Bennett or Tom Jones, redis-covered, rewigged and marketed for a whole new generation, but I don't hold out much hope (singing jazz unplugged ver-sions of 'Bedsitter' – bewildering thought that is – standing, looking perplexed on stage, surrounded by a bevy of young stars, thinking just who the hell are these people . . . just as many of them are wondering the exact same thing about you).

Another aspect of my midlife crisis is that I find myself downsizing, gradually stripping away the flotsam of my life and retaining only those things that have special meaning. Box after box of accumulated stuff is thrown out; pointless objects, books, records, furniture, stuff that I bought when I once had too much money and no doubt under the influence of one substance or another, and felt that I couldn't continue living without acquiring them. Examples of such things might be:

One full-sized stuffed swan
Two papier-mâché Egyptian god figures from the set of
    Dr Who (episode 'Pyramids of Mars')
One nine-foot plaster-cast statue of George slaying the
    dragon
One Gary Glitter stage outfit (not the type of thing one can
    resell any more)
Numerous life-sized toy leopards and tigers
Hundreds of 12-inch singles of every track I ever heard while
    clubbing on drugs, which I bought and then never played
Voodoo masks and occult paraphernalia
One red telephone box
Ten church pews
One altar
One mounted head of a warthog

And so the list goes on.

•

I kept only those things that had sentimental value – photos, letters, gifts. Kept the records I loved, books that influenced and shaped who I am, the ones I always mean to read again one day but never quite get round to it. Midlife means for me taking stock and making space.

And I have made a decision that I will try not to buy new music. There just isn't time in my life any more for experimentation with anything new. Better to stick to what I know than expend valuable time searching for something that at best will only be as good as what I already know I like. I feel I probably have all the music in my collection that I'm ever going to love or that means something to me, and since everything is derivative nowadays, why bother. I've too often been urged to listen to the latest group hailed as something new only to find that I've heard it all before. And I certainly don't want to be one of those older artists desperately trying to align themselves with the latest young hip kids – it's cynical and a bit, well, dare I say it, creepy. I would like to think I might have influenced some of the next generation, but that doesn't mean I want to work with them or hang out with them in the hope their credibility might rub off on me.

Except I suppose someone like David Bowie can get away with it because . . . well, he's David Bowie and that's what he's always done and I personally owe him so much that he can do what he wants. But there are other maturing artists who are frankly, dare I say it, embarrassing.

It is hard to sum up any enthusiasm in what is going on musically today. I like to do my own thing, don't need to look for what is or isn't happening, just get on with being me, doing what I do.

My guess is that today's young record buyers won't ever feel the way my generation did about their music. Music was almost the only thing we had. As a young man trapped in Southport, and unsure of my sexuality, all I had was my music and my pent-up frustrations. The only thrill I got was from the underwear pages of the Freeman's catalogue, where men modelled string pants whilst smoking a pipe and holding a globe.

Music was all I had.

Nowadays teenagers have so much to love aside from music, from David Beckham to Gucci sunglasses, from Lara Croft to Kylie Minogue; the Internet alone can provide teenagers with images I couldn't even have imagined in my formative years, thrills that would have had me imprisoned had I expressed them. Sure, they might love Justin or Christina, but it will pass as all modern things do and they'll move on to the next big thing, but they won't love like I loved, their lives won't be changed as mine was, and they won't know that discovering something isn't the same as being exposed to it.

•

Anyway, where was I? Having downsized my life, I am ready to continue my journey, and they say that in order to keep moving forward we constantly return to our past. So with trepidation I get a train and head towards it.

Southport.

My dear departed grandpa was a sentimental soul and would get all tearful when 'Hold My Hand (I'm a Stranger in Paradise)' by Perry Como would come on the radio. Grandpa loved to sing it to me when he walked holding my hand down on the beach to ease my asthmatic breathing. I guess that is where my sentimentality came from and my singing voice: those long windswept hours on the desolate shoreline. It is my romantic side that vies with my cynical side, but it works. After all, isn't the cynic little more than a disillusioned romantic?

I think of my grandpa and my dear grandma, ending up

in one of the foreboding old people's homes that are abundant in Southport. Old converted mansions with chilly rooms, creaking doors, rose-painted landings with floral-papered rooms. They always smell of old age – of musty supplements, medication and boiled cabbage. I see Grandma still in my mind as she sits in a corner, stooped over the radio, a shrivelled figure with wispy baby-down hair, shoulders wrapped in rugs, her long porcelain fingers under-lining words, reading and rereading the well-wishing cards and studying the old family photos. My grandma struggled for years, but old and frail herself gave in, and did what was best for both of them, and left Grandpa one day in the nursing home. As Alzheimer's took hold she said farewell to the man she once knew.

> We break our backs,
> then our hearts, and we all have to take that long walk
> all leave something behind.

Grandma was a wise kind lady, popular and respected, elegant and lucid. She too became, as one day we all will, a figure in a corner, waiting for that day of judgement, when the plot lines of our lives will be neatly tied. Increasingly losing her sight, her comfort was the radio and speaking books; blindness deprived her of the TV and of faces – faces of loved ones. This once bright informed wise woman, my grandmother, who had shaped me into what I was and am, condemned now to darkness, her bones arthritic and brittle, barely able to lift a china cup. I would never have said it but there really isn't a God for me.

But they aren't, are they, the plot lines of our lives? Not neatly tied up.

I suppose she had a great ninety-six years, which is quite an age. Probably the life she lived was the best that could be managed, better than expected, I bet. She saw the world change: the two Great Wars, a lifetime's work, the Space Shuttle, saw in a new millennium and waved goodbye to life.

Perhaps my biggest regret, and something that gives me terrible guilt, is that I didn't go home for her last Christmas, through some excuse or other. I should have guessed it could have been her last, but having been there all my life, I took it for granted she always would be. Only when they are gone does the reality begin to sink in and regrets take shape.

•

Southport was a place I felt I needed to revisit once again, walk a little in my old footsteps. I always make a short visit at Christmas, ironically never missing even after Grandma passed. Nothing like Christmas to command the present. I have such strong memories of my childhood Christmases, so vivid.

> We all live in houses made of memories and sweet
>   wrappers.
> The unique smell of Christmas, of roasts and pine needles.

I took a walk down onto the beach, or nature reserve as it is now officially known. More desolate and overgrown than I remembered it, wild gorse and long grass, sheltered ponds that teem with life in spring, the last refuge of some endangered species of toad. Walking towards the sea the vegetation fades away from the sandy beach, which stretches down towards the breaking tide.

The beach is now out of bounds for visitors who must not stray from the designated pathways. The beach seems to represent so much about Southport for me, a town trying to reinvent itself, putting paid to the wilderness of its yester-year image whilst trying to control the oncoming tide of change and apathy. I walk past the newly built swimming pool and sports complex (situated where the beautiful old outdoor beach pool used to be), and on past the pier currently undergoing restoration – or should that be modernization – and down the boardwalk of fame where I have been honoured with a wooden plaque engraved with my name: MARC ALMOND. It's not exactly the Rock 'n' Roll Hall of Fame but it's something, I suppose.

Who would have thought it?

I often think what life would have been like if I'd listened to my careers officer at school and gone to work for the Corporation. I would be nine years away from retirement now, maybe with my own flat in Southport, a dog and an unsteady relationship. People would stop on the Parade or in the bakery to exchange pleasantries, or wave from the bus as I trundled home. I would be one of the local oddities, quite a character, Sandy's son, runs the local amateur dramatic society, never married, you know. Takes all sorts.

That's how I imagined it would have been for me, as it is for quite a few single men of my age. You stay within walking distance of where you were born, and all those plans of leaving never quite materialize, and then it's too late. Small towns do that if you stall, routine and familiarity comforting, the outside world an increasingly threatening and hostile prospect as the years pass.

Then one day leaving is not an option any longer, there's more behind you than ahead, just as it is for married couples.

> Two kids. Home-loving wife.
> Bit on the side when the occasion arises
> H.P. Nothing fancy. Neat semi.

I think of how lucky I have been, and luck has everything to do with it. You do something that a thousand people tried before but for you it just happens. It doesn't mean anything other than you were just in the right place at the right time. Fortune smiles on you. As a teenager walking across the endless Southport dunes, directionless and uncertain of what to do with my life, how could I ever have imagined that one day I would be the most famous person to come out of Southport (not that there was any serious competition). Sneaking that fag at school behind the boiler room, docking it and slipping the remainder in my pencil tin (I always hated that they tasted of lead after that), how could I have ever imagined that I would meet such people and experience things I wouldn't have dared envisage. I often like to think of moments that I wouldn't have had if I'd gone to work for the council.

For a start I wouldn't have gotten my own plaque on the walk of fame. I'm not talking about the obvious things that success brings, like money and travel, but those moments that I could never have imagined whilst growing up would happen to me.

I walked past the fairground and a new state-of-the-art roller coaster that loops and looms over the run-down Pleasureland like some dinosaur skeleton.

But Southport and I are not what we were, having both seen better days. As time passes we find it hard to keep up.

> Lord Street
> Farnborough Road
> Gainsborough Road
> The Southport Theatre
> Familiar places, silver hair
> Reminiscing in the barber's chair.

On the beach I looked for the area that I used to call Fairyland, a place where gentlemen loitered and approached you for a light or directions, holding eye contact for that fraction too long. The sands have shifted and the scrub is overgrown but I still recognized certain spots, twenty-eight years later still recall the lie of the land. I recognized a tree under which I sat and ate my sandwiches one hot summer afternoon when I was approached by a merchant sailor named Dennis. And looking out to sea I still saw the prawn boats out on the muddy shallows, just beyond the sewage outlet.

Eventually I found myself outside the place where my old school, King George V, stood. It was long since pulled down and replaced by a college but there were the brick marks where the classroom blocks stood, and I could hear that unique sound of children's playgrounds. How foreboding and fearful that school building had seemed, and how small it must have been in reality. The feeling of emptiness that descended on Sundays, knowing that school was the following day, homework deadlines loomed, shops were closed, and the hours seemed turgid and glutinous. By contrast Saturdays were carefree and filled with quality time-wasting, and school seemed far further than a day away.

I think perhaps that wherever we were born, something of that place is part of our make-up, and throughout our lives tries to lure us back to it, calling us, a yearning to return that we cannot ignore. I believe that evolution has pre-programmed this into us; just as eels or salmon are compelled to return, so are we. I found myself asking, what does it all mean, what are the answers, what is the purpose and above all else, who am I? And standing on the pier's hall of fame, I repeated to myself, just who am I? And then, quite by chance, I gazed down and my question is answered on the plaque.

I'm 'Marc Almond'.

•

Leeds.

Of course, everyone knows (obviously not everyone but if you're reading this I assume you will) that after Southport

I moved to Leeds. Now at the time it seemed like the Bright Lights Big City place to me. I went through some of the most pivotal moments of my growing up in Leeds. Even now I have a strong affection for it. It was the place where Soft Cell was formed, and I feel it became a part of me. It holds so many fond memories that I now feel I need to get in touch with them too.

My journey is, as I said, about patterns and tracks, inter-connecting cogs and wheels, of coincidence, which of course is no coincidence. Going to Leeds was destiny, meeting Dave Ball, forming Soft Cell, making the right connections, fate. I call it convergence.

Naturally all of us assume we are playing the lead in our lives, but in reality turn out to be bit-part players in someone else's drama. In my case though I think I got the lead part, of sorts, in something akin to a daytime soap.

Fate was kind to me. It could just as easily seen me leave Leeds disillusioned, packed me back to Southport to working for the council in Highways and Byways where I would have neglected to authorize the dunes as a nature reserve and thereby relegated the endangered toads to extinction, their spawn collected by goofy boys and condemned to jam jars before being flushed down the toilet.

It's fate. For the toads and me.

•

I discovered that most of my old haunts in Leeds were still there. Cities 'up North' don't usually change too much; maybe a lick of paint or the addition of a pool table, but nothing too radical. Leeds, though, was the exception to this rule. It has gone upmarket, including the addition of a Harvey Nichols and the 'hip as it gets whilst not actually being hip' Malmaison Hotel. The source of this new-found affluence is hard to determine, since little else appears to have changed.

I was relieved to discover the Warehouse club is still going and despite a name change, nothing much else has. In fact I found it a bit overwhelming standing by the same coat check where I had once worked. Almost at once the years dissolve, and I'm back there, can see myself snorting cheap speed, applying more make-up in a compact mirror, dancing to disco, shouting at drunken rent boys and feeling like 'all the world can go to bloody hell' in my new Romantic X-clothes gear, snakebite in one hand and fag in the other.

Walking around the Corn Exchange towards Briggate I saw the doorway that led into Charlie's, Leeds' first gay club, now gone, replaced coincidentally by a new gay cafe, one of many gay venues that have sprung up (breweries have realized 'there's money in them there gays'). I was relieved to see the New Penny pub is still open, still as rough and intimidating as ever, hosting those endangered Northern drag antiquities who still refer to Jools & Sand (brings a smile to my dolly old eek and makes my lallies tremble), the price of fish, and mime to Petula Clark songs.

I took a car before I left and got the driver to take me down old familiar streets. We passed the basement where I wrote the song 'Say Hello Wave Goodbye', down Leicester Grove where 'Bedsit' was written; through Harehills, the area where the Yorkshire Ripper had struck and I remembered that collective fear the city had; through the red light areas where women still desperately ply their trade.

Driving past the Polytechnic I was relieved to see the Faversham pub still open and the Coberg, my old student haunts. Past the Phonographique club where I DJ'd for a while before being sacked and banned after a drunken fight. It was never the same after I left, I was told, and that at least gave me some satisfaction. Not long after that I became famous, and that too gave me some satisfaction. Hell, to be honest, it gave me loads.

'Criticism comes easier than creativity'
– Zeuxis, 400 BC

•

Travelling back to Leeds and Southport helped me understand a little of this midlife malaise that I am suffering.
Revisiting old places brought back memories I had all but
forgotten, memories that came back into existence as though
to facilitate a journey. Remembering who I was before I was
what I became.

Having arrived back from Leeds feeling more positive
about my life, encouraged by an attitude of 'life is what you
make it' and an invite to a high-profile opening of the Saatchi
Gallery, I began to think life wasn't over. They still considered
me a contender: Saatchi Gallery invite, a serious artist happening event, not to be sniffed at. Normally of course I never
attend anything despite my management reminding me that
'out of sight is out of mind', and assured that this was something extremely exclusive I agreed to go, and set off.

I arrived, down the red carpet, posed for the photographers and in. So there I was inside, trying to look interested
in the art pieces whilst discreetly surveying the room to see
who else was there, and what level of celebrity I was in
contention with. Remember, regardless of your status, more
famous celebrities elevate you by their presence, but lesser
ones demote you, dragging you down to their level. While
pondering the meaning of a giant plastic ashtray filled with
ciggie butts, I suddenly saw a familiar face – I panicked.
Carol Vorderman – what was she doing here? I suspected
this might not be as exclusive as I was led to believe, but
convinced myself her being here might just be an oversight.

Oh God. Glancing over my shoulder I noticed Mariella Frostrup. I could feel myself breaking out in hives, a single rivulet of sweat running down my back. She was standing right behind me, and we were both looking at the same piece: a stained mattress with two strategically placed melons and a bucket.

I was sweating because she might remember what I said about her in my last book, which was not too flattering. I think, if she says hello then I'll say hello, but I'm not saying hello first, but she really was engrossed in the art so I sidled off. That was a close one.

Then I noticed Michael Grade and felt a little relieved. After all he is, if not famous, a quality guest so I loitered around near him. But my relief was short-lived: just as I was pretending to find some meaning in an eight-foot pile of dead plastic mice, my heart sank. I spotted an actress from *Footballers' Wives*, an actor from *Hollyoaks* or *Family Affairs* and finally a face from *Celebrity Fit Club*. I felt deflated and claustrophobic. What the hell was I doing there? I headed for the nearest exit, stepping over a figure in a sleeping bag in the foyer: one of the art pieces. I cursed myself for having gone.

I didn't want to be a celebrity; I wanted to be an artist.

And then it occurred to me that part of my midlife crisis stems from what is expected of me in order to achieve what I wanted, and what I want.

> I don't know the key to success –
> but the key to failure is trying to please everybody.

9

Germany

STOP! NON-EROTIC CABARET

•

Throughout my career Germany has proved a valuable market for me, and still does. Over the decades I have visited it countless times, and formed many enduring memories. It seems then only appropriate to return and dig over those old ghosts, and see what, if anything, I can glean from the past to find some meaning in my present. After all, my degrading experience at the Saatchi opening had left me deflated.

Of all the countries of Europe Germany is perhaps the most complex, and the German people the most alienable; a country whose past has indelibly scarred the present. On the blackboard of history wiped clean, the chalk outlines remain forever legible. Having spent so much time in Germany, talking to people, one begins to understand a little of how difficult it is to be German, for them to find a national pride and place in a world that refuses to forgive or forget the past. Not that I am saying it should be forgotten, but for the postwar generations of Germans who inherited the sins of their forefathers, it must seem terribly unfair.

In modern Germany much of the past remains conspicuous by its absence. What is done cannot be undone, and therefore best not spoken of or dwelt on, seems to be part of the collective psyche. It's not an easy nation to understand;

Germans are guarded and sceptical of outsiders. Emotion has been superseded by efficiency, methodical and techno-cratic, and in so doing they have perhaps lost a little of their humanism. For me the industrial electro pioneers of the seventies, the group Kraftwerk, could only have come out of Germany – cold, industrial automatons, the music entirely devoid of emotion, minimal and machine-driven.

Throughout the ensuing decades, and considering the size of its population, culturally Germany has remained stifled by its preoccupation with technological perfection. What I'm trying to say, and not that well I suspect, is that it's not setting the world alight culturally, which doesn't bode well regarding my success there.

•

So my self-esteem was at an all-time low, but life goes on, midlife crisis or not. I found myself once more in Berlin to film a video. The only thought that keeps me going is that I'm still in demand, required to star in a video promo for a track I collaborated on with Dutch producer and DJ Ferry Corstan called 'Soul On Soul'. (Now forget all that business I mentioned earlier about mature artists collaborating with younger ones. It was nonsense, I was ranting.)

Since the budget for the video was £150,000 I figured somebody must still be interested in me. The director talked me through the storyboard, which involved me being filmed singing to the track while standing precariously on top of various Berlin landmarks.

I nodded agreeably.

Up for anything and before you know it I was standing on the roof of the Sony Centre, a Soviet-style skyscraper hotel in east Berlin, and on top of the golden angel-like figure that appears to float over the city – Siegessaule – the Victory column, which every film and video maker uses (though which victory it represents I can't imagine). Up there, lording it up, helicopter filming me, I was the star again, but a star with a budget, which is how I felt it was always meant to be.

Ferry, being on the shy side, preferred to take a back seat in the performing, leaving it all to me, and of course I was happy to oblige. This was about the most important person I knew – me. I forgot about middle age, forgot about my crisis, lost in the fabulousness of it all – I'd achieved perfect humility. But who was I fooling?

The video was eventually shown on rotation on MTV Europe and topped some European dance charts for weeks on end. It felt like I was back ... Well, kind of! I told everyone the track was number one and it was ... in the Dutch charts for several weeks (which obviously I failed to mention). Then Ferry went off to the Far East and the track didn't get released in England, and the record company cut their losses and moved on.

I had been so sure it would be a huge hit, but what did I know?

God just wants to take a piss on my parade at every opportunity. Serves me right for enrolling in the Church of Satan for a cheap theatrical thrill all those years back.

•

Since Germany was one of the places I still sold records, and after having that taste of success, I agreed to do a duet with the German band Rosenstolz, a cover of the late great Klaus Nomis' 'Total Eclipse'. Wonderful Klaus – I had met him many years before back in New York. Oh, those early eighties Danceteria days. Our version had a mad video to accompany it with me dressed in a punk style, dancing in Klaus style as a tribute. With a Germanic beat and Wagnerian chorus I had to keep my right arm in check. More importantly it was a Top Twenty hit, and I was feeling better, and everything was suddenly going to plan.

Until . . .

Rosenstolz and I found ourselves performing 'Total Eclipse' on the German Eurovision song show – the show in which the public choose the official entry to represent Germany in the international Eurovision. I would like to point out that we were not entering the competition but were providing a 'musical interlude' (I assured myself with extreme irony) while the winner was decided by the German voting public.

But backstage I began to have serious reservations about agreeing to participate. Now if you thought the actual Eurovision was tacky, try to imagine what the qualifying contest (especially for Germany) was like. It was a procession of performers who were, quite frankly, shocking. I was Marc Almond, serious artist, or so I thought; so what was I doing on this show? I kept telling myself I was being ironic, but irony is an acquired taste – where one man sees irony another might just see desperation. Is this what trying to find a way out of my mid-life crisis had led me to? I hid in my dressing room, watching the proceedings on a monitor, a procession of performers taking to the stage, my toes curling so uncomfortably I felt like demanding a pair of Aladdin slippers.

The final performer eventually (and I mean eventually) took to the stage. The show started at the bottom and worked its way down. Then it suddenly hit an all-time low. My jaw slackened and hit the floor. Now I've seen some things in my travels but I've never seen anything like this and, worse still, never had to follow it on stage. His name was Rudolph Mooshammer, a Bavarian designer/performer/ socialite who looked not unlike Liberace (except he made Liberace look like Ray Winstone). His skin was an industrial-orange-rust colour, his hair dyed jet black in a bouffant, and he was wearing a seventeenth-century velvet suit with ruffs. He then mimed to an electro disco track called 'Teilt Freud und Lied' that sounded like it was recorded on a Bontempi. Needless to say he didn't win. I was later informed that, up until a few years back, he had never been seen in public unless escorted by his mother (who had since died). His bestseller, entitled 'Mama und Ich', documents their 'unusual' closeness. Now Rudolph's only companion is his miniature pampered dog called Daisy whom he carries around at all times in an alligator-skin handbag, he even published a book (entitled *Ich, Daisy*), which includes Daisy's favourite recipes. Needless to say his sexuality remains a closely guarded secret. Yeah, right!

As I headed out of my dressing room towards the stage, I passed Mooshammer in the corridor, minions minioning around him, smiling for photographers in several irony-free poses.

Afterwards, sitting in my hotel room in Berlin I felt miserable. Middle-aged and humiliated and miserable. But at least I was being miserable in the Hyatt Hotel, which is expensive and luxurious, and most importantly, paid for.

·

Love like you've never been hurt, work like you don't need the money and dance like no one is watching.

Over the past decades two cities in Germany have been very special places for me. First of course is Berlin. I first came when it was still an island in the Soviet sea. I remember the tensions of early visits, Bowie's Low in my head, the West thumbing its neon nose at the East, and the East glowering back with those old red eyes, disdainful and defiant.

When the Wall came down, I remember some West

Berliners smiling through gritted teeth, wary that their unique position would be somehow lost. And in some ways it was.

Since German unification, Berlin has become vast, sprawling, and now redevelopment has blurred the boundaries. Even after all these years I still can't get my bearings. It seems a city without a defined centre. And inevitably it is East Berlin that has become hip and happening, where all the fashionable clubs and bars are found, where the scene's faces are seen and artists have migrated.

The film *Cabaret* had been such an influence in my early life, inspired so many feelings and fuelled so much hope that if people make art like that there is hope. So when I was offered the chance to perform Chanson cabaret in Berlin I felt it might fulfil something in me. The club where I was to perform was called Big Eden, owned by the 72-year-old Berlin playboy Rolf Eden, famous in the German capital for his countless number of sex partners. Rolf recently came up with an unusual offer to lure women into his bed by promising that the last woman he sleeps with will get his inheritance of about $244,000. Applicants must be beautiful and preferably under 30.

The club had been a seventies Playboy playground, red velvet kitsch, subdued lighting and gold gilt.

Perfect.

This once-happening haunt had lost its hipness, and the organizers felt my appearance would help restore some of its former glory – I was the honey to attract the bees, it seemed, or should that be pollen, whatever. And I was in Berlin anyway, so I agreed.

So I was in the dressing room applying more and more make-up, thinking this is what I should be doing, this is Marc Almond territory. Not Eurotrash, or dance, but this, Chanson – cabaret – Brel – thoughts of any crisis alleviated.

Then the promoter barged in and informed me, 'No one comes here any more but it should be OK tonight.'

So I asked if they had sold any tickets.

'No, we don't sell tickets. They have to pay on the door. But I'm sure it will be packed. We even had someone enquire from Prague about it an hour ago.'

With that she disappeared.

Oh, that's just great, I'm thinking. I felt wary. Still there were a couple of hours to go, so why worry about your hair when your head's been cut off. And besides, maybe the enquirers from Prague have hired a private jet and are actually on their fucking way here. Still, ever the professional I applied some more make-up and tried to focus, and think of the money. And I only had to play for twenty minutes, so how bad can it be?

No, don't tempt fate.

Then Neal X, my accompanist and guitarist, sauntered in and suggested maybe we should go through a couple of songs in the dressing room as he seemed to have had a bit of a blank. So I'm thinking to myself as he struggled with chord changes that maybe he should have rehearsed, but hell, too late now.

Just think of the money. The Singing Hustler they call me. But being paid well makes anything a little easier, and no matter how bad it is you know it will be over eventually, and let's face it, there are worse jobs in the world (and like the prostitute said, 'It beats waitressing').

Mind you, there are some things that no amount of money can entice me to do and that I have turned down. It usually translates into the more money offered, the greater the humiliation. And believe this or not, quite at the opposite end, there are even occasions when I will do something for nothing if I really want to do it, or if it's artistic or even on the rare occasion for charity.

So it all balances out in the end.

But I'm not going to starve for my art. As you get older the opportunities to work might get less frequent, demand lulls, and healthcare costs or cosmetic procedures just get ever more expensive, and frequent.

I enjoy singing, but more than that I enjoy singing and getting paid for it.

•

So where was I?

The dressing-room door swung open and the promoter announced it was time to go on stage.

As it turned out the place was packed. I need not have worried.

All was going well until halfway through the set, during a quiet intimate song called 'L'Esclave' ('The Slave') – a song about a transvestite slave who wants to get a good old seeing-to by a big old black man, also a slave ... oh, you get the picture? (I imagine you're trying to get that picture out of your head right now.) Anyway, all was quiet and I'm singing, giving it all, emoting and grand gesturing, and what could I hear, a group of people somewhere beyond the lights chatting, oblivious of my performance and just chatting.

I was enraged and stopped the song. Silence. And get this, they went on chatting. I pointed towards them and announced, 'If I'd wanted people to talk throughout I'd have played a fucking wine bar,' the irony that it wasn't far removed from a wine bar entirely escaping me.

That got their attention and a round of applause.

Rule 7: the audience will love you for acting up.

Now all eyes were on me and I began the song again and what did I do, forgot the fucking words, mumbling through it. Still the audience were rapturous.

Leaving the stage the applause was deafening.

Rule 4: leave the audience wanting more.

So what did I do, I stupidly broke that rule and went back out without anything planned and blew it, Neal and I fumbling for a song.

That put me on a downer. I hate encores. When you think about it they are stupid. You know you're going to do one (except in this case), the audience knows you're going to do one, and you haven't done that song yet (the one they all came for) and everyone knows what it is – it's a ridiculous predictable ritual and you know what, I might just stop doing them. Mind you, it's hard to resist.

Afterwards I was informed that the Pet Shop Boys were in the audience and it was Neil Tennant who was chatting through my song, and my tirade was aimed at him. That's OK, I figure, because I talked all the way through their musical. And sniggered. Mind you, not as loudly as Tom Watkins, who, between sniggers, yawned noisily and chatted on his mobile phone. No, I'm joking, hey, guys, I love you both, really.

•

Some final thoughts.

Berlin is the one European city where the lines of the past connect to a reinvented present; it is in the here and now and yet some place else altogether.

The new site of power, it is shadowy and dark beneath glass and chrome. It is cleaned up but not entirely. Hi-tech apartments tower next to run-down squats, sex clubs nestle between global fashion chains and coffee shops, and depravity and technology fill the spaces in between.

New Berlin is an architect's fantasy; though not a clean canvas but one washed over. Travelling through it by car you swiftly move from vastly differing neighbourhoods, feelings emerge of futurism, activism and disenchantment.

One senses that Berlin is a work in progress. The soundtrack of Berlin is Techno.

I think what needs to be said of Berlin probably already has, and better summed up than I could. When I think of Berlin I think of decadent cabarets of the past, heavy leather bars, relentless techno raves, heroin, Bowie, Reed, Pop, and cold industrial art spaces. In fact it was only a matter of time till Marilyn Manson discovered Berlin.

Berlin is an art happening, but one where you never quite know whether it is valid or pretentious, real or imaginary.

I always feel detached from it in a way I find hard to qualify. I suppose what I feel about Berlin is that it lacks passion. It is about penetration, intercourse, fellatio. Never about making love.

•

My second favourite German city is Hamburg.

'Oh yes,' you say, 'and we know why – because of the sleazy old Reeperbahn.'

Well, I assure you, it's more than just seedy peep shows and legalized prostitution; well, not that much more. The city's official line is that the Reeperbahn is Hamburg's second greatest attraction and asset (the first is the port itself). Who are they kidding? This long boulevard is Hamburg's infamous centre of nightlife and lies at the heart of St Paul like a lurid scar. The Mile of Sin.

Hamburg is one of Germany's few port towns, and it shows, attracting as ports do the usual eclectic blend of lowlife and rabble, on the trawl for excesses imaginable.

The place I always love visiting is Herbertstrasse, where plate-glass windows allow the women to display their charms to window shoppers. By city ordinance, this street is only open to men over the age of 18. Any curious female tourists who unsuspectingly wander in find themselves being screamed at by the hookers, screeching German fishwives clad in suspender belts (don't think Marlene Dietrich), gesticulating threateningly.

Less expensive liaisons can be found on the streets near Herbertstrasse: Gunterstrasse, Erichstrasse, Friedrichstrasse, Davidstrasse and Gerhardstrasse. Lots of the women here are from the Eastern Bloc. Cross-dressers, transsexuals, and 'shemales' ply their trade here too. Hamburg has some of the dodgiest tranny hookers in Europe, with the exception of Barcelona.

If it's erotic theatre you're looking for, you'll have to move a few blocks away to Grosse Freiheit, a street whose name appropriately translates as 'Great Freedom'. Any act of sexual expression, with every conceivable permutation, is on show here. Be it erotic, be it unsettling, it's all here, often performed by artists whose barely concealed boredom sometimes permeates the setting in ways that anywhere else would be embarrassing, but here seems merely surreal.

I made a visit to the Eros Centre, four floors of aggressive girls who sit outside cabins trying everything, bar knocking you unconscious, to get you inside, and when you ignore their offers they scream insults at you in German, quite recognizable in any language.

A colleague told me he risked it, entered a cabin and was then confronted with the reality that a hand job was all that was on offer – blow jobs, a fuck or anything else would cost extra. So you thought you paid for a 'round the world' and you haven't even left the airport lounge, so to speak.

On the Reeperbahn there is a small reproduction of Paris's Moulin Rouge, decorated with vibrantly painted billboards of girls in garish, scantily clad outfits. The place has a burlesque feel, and I like it. Inside it is all red velvet and gaudy gilt. I got accosted by eager figures like harpies on ecstasy but, though they smiled those wide smiles, their eyes

were cold and hard. Their long nails made a play for my
groin, scratching me in the process. Well, it was a quiet
afternoon and business wasn't exactly booming. I felt like a
titbit thrown into a tank of sharks. With expert precision
my euros were extracted from my fist and then my pockets.
My reward: a couple of women swivelled around a pole,
gyrating, pouting and posing.

Whatever this is about it wasn't sex, and it was certainly
no fun, though it held a kind of fascination, even for me.
Every minute that passes, it costs. Lap dancing, table dancing
– what a strange concept it is: all titillation, and no relief.
When the money runs out, suddenly so does the attention,
the smiles disappear and you're at once invisible. Wait a
minute; they were my best friends a minute ago.

Outside I strolled in the early evening dusk down the
Reeperbahn, soaking up the atmosphere, reassured that
nothing much has changed over the decades, still the same
old routines played out.

Two German fans photographed me under a vibrant blue
neon sign that said Baby Doll lounge, a European cousin
perhaps of the infamous New York topless go-go bar. It was
one of those moments. Then all of a sudden a little way
down the street a commotion broke out, which almost as
quickly became very nearly a riot. Then the police appeared
and by that time I realized the throng of people were
protesters, making a stand against war or globalization or
such; and for a moment I was almost tempted to roll up my
sleeves and pitch in. Then I spotted in the throng a fire-eater
and juggler, which bode badly, because that meant mime
artists are never far behind. For a moment though I felt like
raising my voice and protesting about something but I'm not
quite sure what. Maybe I've just got protest fatigue; after all
I spent half an hour protesting about the room service earlier
at the Hyatt, and it never really amounted to much.

I moved away from the rioters, down a quiet side street. The rioters too, slipped away into the shadows, away from the lines of police that had now blocked the road in the distance – into the side streets and alleyways, into the bier kellers and kinos, dissolving into the night. Before I knew it I was exploring some of those salubrious places that my publisher insists I visit and document. After being harassed and hassled by the transvestite hookers on Davidstrasse I slipped into the kino. A maze of corridors and booths showing videos in a network of gloomy rooms, flickering lights from the obligatory dusty video screen, only the voices and the noises from the porn films echoing around. People moving in and out of the blackness.

There was no beauty to be found there, only overweight Germans in badly fitting leather pants, pale and balding ghosts with dead eyes. In the centre of the cellar was a collapsed sofa on which lay a couple of young prostitutes, late-teenage street types. One was wearing just a coat over his naked body. They propositioned everyone, sitting up as a potential client neared, their faces pallid and drawn with dark skull eyes, chattering teeth, grinding jaws. But their eyes had lost their sparkle long since, now dull and psychotic.

One noticed me and looked upwards, his face illuminated by the flickering movie. He was on crystal meth amphetamine, offering me a hit of it. I declined. It's an insidious drug. I tried it once and ended up awake for four days, looking like a grinning skull too, my stomach shrunk into a tightened painful fist, and I was a slavering wreck. Crystal meths also makes you very horny, in fact obsessive about sex, but ironically you find you can do very little about the craving. So these two lads had that same exhausted frustrated desperate look, almost feral and dispirited.

I left, to find whatever it was I was looking for some other place.

Further down the main road and up some stairs I found myself in a filthy cinema lounge, greasy torn curtains, brown stains making abstract patterns across the material, another blurred video screen the only light source, and a broken red exit sign. The place was blue with smoke, dope smoke, sweet crack smoke, and another smell, an indeterminable, rancid, gag-inducing smell that I couldn't quite locate. This place had seen better days. I could see figures through the haze, women lounging about, one or two administering blow jobs to elderly rotund gents who moaned and writhed in the broken cinema seats, eyes closed in bliss, or just asleep. Closer inspection made me realize that they were not women at all ('Holy smoke, Batman'), they're, yes you guessed it, transvestites or transsexuals.

My inspection wasn't that thorough.

For a moment I surveyed the car-crash scene.

What at first was curiosity soon turned to depression: I felt neither thrilled nor inspired. What a sad scene it was, and even though I must have seen such similar scenes in the past, I'd never felt the way I did now.

What the hell was happening to me? Was this something new?

•

Out in the air I took a deep breath. The protest had all but fizzled out. I don't need squalor, I need space and air and beauty. You know, there's only so much squalor anyone can take in their lives and I was pretty near my high-water mark. This place was like an evening in watching Christiana F followed by Taxi Zum Clo with a bottle of stale poppers and Blue Nun for company.

I want to hear Marlene Dietrich sing 'Einen Mann'. I want 'Blue Angel', 'Surabaya Johnny' sung by Lotte Lenya, 'Wonderbar' by Zara Leander, Helmut Berger as Ludwig II of Bavaria; even Liza Minnelli singing 'Mein Lieber Herre' would do me right now. German camp. Dirk in his leather coat. I wanted to drink beer and eat those greasy spit-roast chickens at the Oktoberfest. But most of all I just wanted to see a beautiful face:

> Falling in love again?
> I can't help it.

10

Amsterdamned

In the Port of Amsterdam

•

It was a freezing cold February afternoon, overcast as Amsterdam often is, and I was sitting alone in my hotel room at the Marriott – not my usual hotel, the American, which I was told was full. I suspected that wasn't true and had more to do with the budget cuts that had brought this Soft Cell tour I was on down to a shoestring.

Actually the room wasn't bad: it was a suite, clean, and the air conditioning was refreshingly cold; the BBC was reassuringly on the TV, showing Pressburger and Powell's film *The Red Shoes*, a beautifully surreal melodramatic camp fest starring Robert Helpmann and Moira Shearer.

As I lay on the bed constantly ordering room service, and contemplating how my life wasn't all it was cracked up to be, the film finished and a documentary on Rudolph Nureyev followed. Thank God, some light relief; the past two weeks of this tour, filling time in charmless hotel rooms, I had watched nothing but CNN and the endless reports on the War on Terrorism.

It's lonely on tour; the only time you get to be with people is the time you're required to perform, and then it's back to the hotel.

I quite like that in some ways, but this time I found

myself with too much time to dwell on the way I'm feeling about midlife, time to mope around, reassess and generally get myself worked up.

On tour my compulsive-obsessiveness with routine takes over, and I struggle to create order in the chaos. I find myself worrying constantly about my voice holding out, dreading the onset of a throat infection or straining my vocal chords singing a repertoire of songs that no longer suits me, more rock than the usual crooner torch songs I've become more suited to. Then those thoughts – that maybe I'm just too old to be doing this. Maybe I can get away with it for a bit longer with some dignity but it's a long way from those speed- and cocaine-fuelled shows on gruelling tours in cheap hotels of my yesteryear. The irony doesn't escape me that the vocal sound I created on the Soft Cell songs is proving a nightmare to recreate since I learned to sing. I have to take a regime of throat medications, slippery elm tablets and tea-tree gargle before each show, and occasionally Prednisolone steroids when things are looking particularly bad – last-minute emergency measures, I assure you, because the next day my throat can swell up like one of those deadly tree frogs that disappointingly top the most poisonous lists on the world's most dangerous animals programmes.

I find too I have to avoid smoke, and to everyone's delight keep quiet between shows, so being alone with my own company is the best option.

So I take consolation in my tour rider (a tour rider for anyone unsure is a list of requirements I impose as a con-dition of touring, just to get me through). I heard recently that some people in the industry consider me a 'difficult artist', which I take to mean they think I'm unreasonable. This is absolutely unfounded, I assure you. I admit I have particular dietary needs such as no onion, garlic, chives, leeks, spices, et cetera, won't eat any red meat, pre-prepared food, or anything fried or with a heavy sauce. But aside from that, I'll eat pretty much anything, so long as it is organic of course.

I must have cornflakes and ice-cold milk in my dressing room for when I come off stage to settle my stomach, and sliced honeydew melon. It's my stomach, the bane of my life, and IBS, an ulcer, hernia and chronic indigestion that dictate this regime.

Admittedly there are a few idiosyncrasies I require to be supplied such as red towels to take on stage. And that's about it. Red complements the black stage outfits I almost always wear (off-white towels are not a good look).

And regarding hotels, the rumour that I always change hotels upon arriving in any city is in part true, but only because they usually fail to meet up to my exacting standards. Promoters as a matter of course will always try to skimp on hotels if they think they can, and I'm resolute about what I want, so it's out of the car, into the lobby, out of the lobby and back into the car. Then it's the same old yarn about some business conference in the city and all the hotels are full and such, which fails to convince me, until by some miracle they relent and as luck would have it find a suitable hotel that has just had a cancellation. Bullshit smells the same in every language.

I rarely travel on tour with Dave Ball or the crew, who go on the tour bus. I have the excuse that they all smoke and stay up all night drinking and it would be quite impossible for me to keep from losing my voice in such conditions. I fly from city to city or if close by get my own driver. Besides Dave never flies, refusing point blank to get on a plane as he has an acute fear of flying – though oddly enough he overcame it to take Concorde.

•

So here I was on tour, which I don't like that much, and feeling particularly past my best. I knew it would be my last major one: I had no choice. As Soft Cell, our reunion come and all but gone, we were now playing the final dates of our European tour that were scheduled for the previous year but cancelled in order that I could have my hernia operation. We were fulfilling our commitments as we were legally obliged to do, and I felt a bit like I was going through the motions. The thrill had gone, the album came and went, the single had made the Top 40 and we'd appeared on *TOTP* which felt very odd after so many years, but rewarding. But it all happened so fast, and like a dud firework the blue touchpaper went out.

Now we were finishing off the tour across Europe, in those grey towns you could only hazard a guess were in which country, and in venues that seemed to be getting dingier with each passing appearance. The shows on the whole had gone well, though it was a struggle to muster any enthusiasm.

As I looked out of my Amsterdam hotel window, counting the days till I got home, the lights twinkled on the canals but failed to brighten my spirit. It hadn't always been like that; let's go back less than three years. Cue slow dissolve, and echoey voice-over.

•

Dave and I were waiting backstage at Ocean, the brand new state-of-the-art music venue in East London. It was the opening night and we were the special guests invited to launch it (and relaunch Soft Cell), and over successive nights have concerts there. It was the first time we had appeared together on stage in seventeen years and a coup for the venue; it was a chance for us to gauge the interest in making an album. Both of us were painfully aware of the eighties revival that was happening, that always seemed to be happening since the end of the eighties; from Romo through to Electroclash, we were cited as inspirations for them all.

But the bandwagon was pulling out and everyone was clambering on board, something Dave and I didn't want to do. We preferred instead to do our own thing, simply look on hoping that we retained at least some credibility and would avoid the crash when the whole thing calamitously skidded off the road.

But backstage, then, it had seemed, in that moment, the right thing to do, something in the air. We would write some songs and record a new album, and call ourselves Soft Cell again. After all, when we were performing or writing together we were Soft Cell as far as everyone else was concerned.

Ocean was packed. Waiting backstage you could feel the buzz from out front. I looked at Dave, smartly dressed in his suit, nervously twitching, and he smiled one of those what the hell are we doing sort of smiles, and as the doors to the stage slipped open dry ice engulfed us and we calmly walked out.

'Tonight, Mathew, we're going to be Soft Cell!'

•

The crowd loved us, the critics raved about us, and Soft Cell was reborn and re-energized instead of rehashed and retread.

Then it all fell into place and seemed to follow on naturally, except at some point something happened, one of those turning points when you suddenly know this isn't how it was planned, when it becomes clear to you that no matter which way you look at it, no matter how much you ponder it or turn it around in your hand, that last colour on the Rubik's cube is on the wrong side.

The order of events was planned as follows:

A Soft Cell greatest hits album released with two brand new bonus tracks, followed by a brand new album and single, short tour, promotion schedule to boost the single into the chart and hey presto, hit single, hit album, everyone overwhelmed and we're flavour of the month. If nothing else it was a plan. It seemed like it could work. Stranger things have happened.

Midlife crisis? What was that about?

•

The new album entitled *Cruelty Without Beauty* fulfilled all my expectations, and I was extremely proud of the songs. The theme was life in the new millennium: our twisted celebrity culture, sleaze, consumerism, sensationalism, mid-life fears, darkness and immorality, all wrapped up in infec-tious melodies and understated arrangements. Throughout recording fans sent in messages hoping it would sound like this particular album or that one from our past, most unsure just what they wanted. In the end we did what we always had and pleased ourselves.

The press reviews ranged from fantastic through to good, though apparently there were a few less than glowing ones that I of course paid no heed to. The high point came when we played to a sold-out Brixton Academy the week the single charted at number 39 (not as high as the record company had hoped) but we decided to wait and see what happened.

The single sales the following week began to indicate the record would go no higher unless we agreed to appear on some or other TV show. We agreed. But then the goalposts moved: the TV shows would only have us on if we sang 'Tainted Love'.

We didn't agree. Absolutely not!!

We were promoting our new single, not 'Tainted Love'.

So the TV show never happened because I refused to

trade my past for a shot at the present. Besides I know that old trick, you do 'Tainted Love' and then find that any reference to the new single has been edited out because the woman with the largest collection of Franklin Mint thimbles ran over time. In fact I'm never going to sing it on TV again.

•

As I said, the plan for our comeback faltered and the single went down. The album was released but early signs were ominous. The thing is that though each of us believes ourselves to be the centre of the world, the reality is that we're not the centre of anyone else's, or at least not in enough numbers. That part of the plan about actually selling records, you know, that really important part of the plan, faltered too.

Sure we were selling albums but just not enough.

Then there was, in the midst of all this, a Soft Cell US tour, which was mostly, but not all, bad. Half of the tour was cancelled at the last minute – freezing weather, imminent war – 'We're just not selling enough tickets in some of the mid-American towns,' said the promoter. 'I wish it were different, but everyone's feeling the squeeze since 9/11.'

Everything became the fault of 9/11. Shares plummeted, the album didn't sell, the dog died, blah, blah, blah.

I could live with not going there anyway. The timing was all up to cock. We went to do *Breakfast USA* to announce our tour, which didn't happen till seven months after that appearance, so I guess most people had forgotten. The segment of the show we were scheduled to appear on, which I discovered five minutes prior to recording, was entitled 'One Hit Wonders'. No one had told me because everyone knew I would have turned it down. Too late, I had to bite my lip and everyone assured me it had huge ratings. When asked by the host how it felt to be a One Hit Wonder, I replied, if you're gonna have one hit in the USA then it might as well be the biggest of all time. In the UK the term One Hit Wonder is used in a derogatory way; in America it is quite different, because it's at least one reason to celebrate a career success.

In honesty I would have liked to have cancelled the whole thing, but Dave Ball was somewhere in the mid-Atlantic on a Pakistani cargo ship eating curry for every meal and couldn't be contacted (remember, he doesn't fly). The tour stumbled ahead and those dates that we did manage to play pleased the fans – LA and New York were two of the best shows we ever did. The shows that never went ahead disappointed and angered fans. The tour lost a small fortune.

After that not much went right, which eventually led me to the hotel room in Amsterdam playing at the arse end of Europe to fulfil our commitment and to deal with the losses. Smoky venues, with three lights (bulbs in tin cans) and cheap sound systems and last year's backdrops.

Déjà vu to you too!

•

Amsterdam is, like Hamburg, one of those cities that musicians on tour love to visit. A 'must stopover' stopover. The hash cafes, dope shops, space cakes, and the prostitution and nightlife. It is the one city where bands can suffer the most as they are all usually too fucked up and hung over to play. Days off on tour usually coincide with Amsterdam.

In fact it was one of the first overseas cities I visited in my teens, taken by an older sponsor. The kind of place where older gentlemen could impress their protégés, especially in the seventies. In fact looking around today you still see them accompanied by youthful acolytes, more often than not sitting in the windows of the coffee houses, both lost in their separate worlds, rarely exchanging words since arguing on the plane over.

Amsterdam is a playground, a great place to be on your own or with independent friends as there is so much to do. It is not a place to take the 'other half' as temptation places a terrible strain. There are plenty of chances for furtive seedy liaisons, though back in my teens chaperoned by my host I felt only pent-up frustration.

It was several years later, I suppose, on the recommendation of my friend Jacques Brel, that I really took the plunge and returned. He told me, 'In Amsterdam there is a sailor,' in fact many sailors, drinking, dancing, sleeping, dying and pulling whores. But I never really found them.

I mainly found drugs and drug users, dope heads, crack addicts, spotty adolescents on the run, leather-clad clones with prolapsed arses hanging out of their chaps, transsexuals, aggressive Eastern European pimps, pushers and crooks, and of course ambling tourists looking around the art museum, torture museum, sex museum and Anne Frank's attic, but then finding themselves in the red-light district, sniggering and blushing.

Amsterdam is a really beautiful city. Sometimes I forget how much affection I have for it, with its glassy canals, crooked toy houses, twinkling lights across arched bridges, and those alleys that glow red and ultraviolet.

The smells too, of fries and mayonnaise, of sugared crêpes and stale beer.

I always forget how small it is and with each subsequent visit it seems to get smaller still, along I suppose with my expectations, until they became almost Lilliputian.

A couple of hours and you've done it, end to end.

It's a working city and now on this visit on a tour that's full of disillusionment, Amsterdam lifts my spirit and makes me smile. Of course bands come here for the dope, as I suspect do most English tourists under thirty. You see their eyes light up in disbelief that coffee shops actually sell it, actually give you a menu of different varieties and strengths, and serve enticing pieces of cake and sticky-looking coconut-covered sweets, richly laced with it.

Of course there is only so much you can smoke or eat and us Brits will usually make ourselves ill within several hours of arriving in the city, rolling joint after joint, the whole weekend dissolving into a haze, and before you know it we are back at Heathrow (having forgotten about that half-used slab of hash in our rucksack), looking sweaty and off colour, only to be pulled aside by a customs officer asking, 'Sir, where have you just come from? Would you mind opening your bag, sir?'

That way they say '*sir*', slightly disdainfully, much like newsreaders say the word 'homosexuaaaal'.

No thanks, you can keep your hash, grass, your temple ball and the whole rest of it. No thanks, not for me any more. I can understand those people who like a joint to calm down at the end of the day, but when you wake up, roll up just to get up, it's time to re-evaluate your life.

You see dope heads everywhere as they sit around apathetically, unmotivated, usually in groups, unkempt and grubby: rolling, munching, giggling, fiddling, braiding, discussing the meaning of the Soup Dragon's role in the Clangers, surrounded by rubbish and paraphernalia. The coffee shops are full of them, in multi-coloured outfits, eyes glazed, rocking back and forth to some distorted reggae beat, from early afternoon to early morning, or until they pass out.

Having said all that, which sounded I suppose like a rant, I still feel it should be legalized in Britain. I don't buy any of the arguments that soft drugs lead to hard drugs, and I feel freedom of choice is the most important thing of all. Let's face it, it takes dope heads all their time and effort to even get out of the house and buy more of it! They love being on downers, even the whole rolling ritual plays a part. Uppers or speedier drugs might encourage them to actively do something. So why not legalize it. In fact legalize all drugs. Just so long as they don't do them in front of me or in public where children might see them and feel the need to run out and jack up – no sir-ee!!!

Personally I was never one for natural highs – what's that all about, like tantric sex, what a load of nonsense.

So dope and Amsterdam go together, a match made in hashish heaven.

I just love to walk around the city. It's something I have to spend a great deal of time doing looking for a decent restaurant. Not an easy place to get a quality meal, but I compromise or I'd starve: at the American Hotel I sit over-looking the main square, and the menu though not great is OK, and variable. In reality it is one of those new generation of fast-food outlets masquerading as a restaurant – you know the type, goat's cheese on arugula with balsamic dressing – but it's not really quality. Or sea bass in fennel sauce with minted new potatoes – microwaved, pre-pack-aged and adequate.

Fast food and Amsterdam go together, a match made in hamburger heaven.

Perhaps there are just too many tourists flooding in and out, and the dodgy edgy quick on-the-make ploy of feed and fleece them at every chance. Amsterdam can be so ruthless, so jaded, but then can't we all?

There is something here for everyone, not much admit-tedly per person, but something of something. No more so than on the sexual front – no deviancy not catered for. However extreme.

For example, I saw advertisements plastered around on walls for an upcoming scatological party, which I hear are getting increasingly popular. I really don't want to have to tell you about them and I am sure they leave nothing to the imagination. Even for the normally transparent excuse of research I couldn't bring myself to visit it, so you'll have to be spared all the odious nutty details. I studied the poster which showed a couple wearing gas masks using another woman as one might use a toilet bowl, though the finer details are left to the imagination. The girls in the poster (I say girls but I really mean hardened old hags) were the types I'd seen in porno flicks dealing with similar subject matter. One comes to mind, a quite distasteful little movie where a woman used a live eel dildo-style on herself, before chopping it in half and frying it in a pan, but oddly enough that wasn't the weird bit: she then squatted over the fried eel in the pan and evacuated an enormous stool into it. Titles. FIN. It certainly covered quite a diversity of themes.

It really isn't for the faint of heart. You can see some stomach-churning sights in this city, but you have to know where to look. The extreme video I've just described doesn't seem that many train stops from station Snuff, from putting body parts in bin bags and dumping them in several different areas of some gloomy forest.

Amsterdam's beloved red-light district looked at first the same as ever; only the faces of the hookers have changed, on rotation it seems. I love to walk down the side alleys where they sit in the windows like some latter-day torch singers, replete in lingerie, all but ready for their gin-soaked finale, winking, a curled finger beckoning, 'thinking of the dollar as they try to tease'.

Or those older ones, bored with the passing world, like old overweight apes that squat in the corner of the ape house, bellies hanging down, unmotivated by the taps on the glass from the curious. Occasionally they might glance up, faces frozen, cold with disinterest. Others, younger ones, are more enthusiastic, smiling the smile of the hard-working hooker, toying with nylon baby-doll nighties, eager to feed a fix, sucking a finger, fingering pearls with pink talons, coaxing drunken men into their red rooms for an imitation of sex.

Tourists stand in front of the windows of girls, clucking and clicking cameras, laughing and drunkenly daring each other forward.

But the sex shop windows I noticed have changed, toned down from what I remembered. No more pictures of the actual act of sex, mainly displays of novelty dildos and cock rings, useless sex aids and impractical novelty toys, fur handcuffs, and all types of gelatinous lubrication in a myriad of acidic colours. Videos have made way for DVDs, and magazines are in short supply and less varied. It seems that even one of the world's most infamous red-light districts has toned itself down, carefully aware that tourists may want to be stimulated and titillated but not entirely disgusted and appalled.

Looking around at Amsterdam's so-called tourist attractions, aside from the sex industry and the hash, it's a pretty poor show. If you're visiting Amsterdam for more than say thirty hours you'll find time on your hands and may feel tempted to visit one of the attractions; I say attractions for want of a better word. The Erotica Museum: what can I say about it? It's on five floors. I went, I walked around, I left. It filled an hour.

Or the Torture Museum, which is a rather sanguine affair. Quite cleverly the torture was the experience of the visit itself, and watching tourists marvel at the inventiveness of the instruments of suffering.

Then there is the Anne Frank house, which is quite the

saddest place. I listened to an American wheelchair-bound tourist outside complaining about the lack of disabled facilities at the museum. With hindsight it would have been more considerate of her to hide on the ground floor.

•

I visited the famous old gay bars and clubs, all situated a short distance from each other. Most have been there since the seventies, feeling a little like Jurassic Park as the old dinosaurs roam hungrily from one to another, looking for yet another tourist to gorge themselves on. I am referring in particular to the leather scene, centred around the famous Argos bar or the Eagle, the Cuckoo's Nest or the Web, patronized by old leather queens who have somehow avoided or managed to live with the Aids crisis. In many other European cities, a thriving leather scene has reinvented itself for a younger crowd. But not Amsterdam – it has lumbered from decade to decade and staggered begrudgingly into the twenty-first century.

The leather queens, some of whom I recognized from visits years earlier, which in itself is a miracle, seem to be preserved in aspic. They wait like leather lizards or praying mantis for a new fresh influx of tourists. But the Dutch seem just too serious and intellectual to actually enjoy sex. Not in that way that Germans seem serious and clinical about it, but you feel the Dutch overanalyse every chance encounter, searching for some meaning, unlike the French who search for deeper meaning and never neglect the passion. And living in the city dedicated to tourist pleasures has left them a bit spoiled and jaded. Each conquest is nothing more than just a stepping stone to another.

This is not Brel's Amsterdam; more accurately the lyrics of his song 'Next' sum it up and I never did want to be Next.

As I strolled down the street past the leather men posing outside the bars, the occasional one not unlike a Tom Of Finland drawing, I noticed that many of them seem to have rather large packets. Apparently the Dutch are meant to have some of the largest penises in the world. I read that while I was waiting in my doctor's surgery.

Amsterdam is a place I could imagine myself living in, being a bit of a dinosaur myself. It's dirty yet romantic, romantic yet sleazy, magical and earthy – in particular I love those houseboats. It is such a sensible country too: tolerance to euthanasia, healthcare and just no-nonsense practical measures.

•

I decided to end my tour with a quick pad around an infamous night sauna on Kerkstraat. Always a Fellini-esque experience, walking past the rows of cabins of semi-illuminated figures and sexual tableaux, and into the murky void of the back room where things squelch underfoot and between toes. A sort of amniotic fluid, one imagines, the beginning of a new life form. My head began to throb in the haze of marijuana and the overpowering waft of amyl nitrate: the obligatory eighties soundtrack, this time early Kylie – 'I Should Be So Lucky'. Indeed?

I wanted to cringe and hide in the shadows as suddenly 'that' song came through the sound system. Good God, it's enough that I had to sing it out on stage on this tour – is there to be no escape? I couldn't shake my head clear of the effects of the marijuana. Round and round I traipsed, past cabins, down twisting corridors, until I eventually bumped into a not unattractive man, and from what I said earlier he was obviously Dutch. We exchanged glances, moved around each other cautiously like two phosphorescent fish in the coral, before he pulled me towards him, spat in my face and grabbed my buttocks with both hands – then suddenly in my head I heard David Attenborough's hushed voice-over: 'This courtship, this prelude to love-making forms a bond.'

Suddenly I wasn't in the mood. I felt tired, deflated, jaded, stoned and more than a little annoyed at being slapped and grabbed. I slapped him back across the face. He backed off, startled.

I walked away empowered. He followed beseechingly and tried to apologize.

Back at the Marriott Hotel I made myself a camomile tea and a bowl of cornflakes, half watching the news.

Tomorrow would be another concert day, some town outside of Amsterdam – Tilburg. I tried not to dwell on it. At least today I had reacquainted myself with this city a little and killed time. That's what touring is about, killing time.

It reminds me of the retired prostitute who confessed, exhausted, 'It isn't the sex, it's the stairs.'

11

Rome: Caligula Syndrome

Paradise Found Is Paradise Lost

•

Rome. Coming to Rome seemed quite the right thing to do to seek a spiritual answer to these feelings of midlife despair. After all, millions of people make pilgrimages to it and come away, if not fulfilled, at least with a plaster cast Christ lamp or Resurrection snow globe.

Surely Rome is the city of pleasure palaces, the ancient and grand decadence of Nero, Caligula and Tiberius. Now Tiberius, there was an emperor! Anyone who attaches fish bait to their own genitals to be nibbled off by carp is a man after my own heart. When all the pleasures have been exhausted, bring out Caligula, along with Gilles de Rais, Torquemada, Hitler, Stalin, Peter (and Catherine) the Great, Louis XIV.

I love history, it is so full of fascinating facts, and I particularly love Rome because it's so full of history. When I'm there I can practically feel the spirit of Caligula surging through my veins at the very sight of those old ruins. I love dictators. If camp is defined by grand gestures with small meaning or failed seriousness, then dictators are camp – oh, come on. Just put out of your mind the appalling atrocities and look at Hitler and Stalin: if they weren't camp then who is, and Saddam Hussein, who had an art gallery dedicated to

portraits of his favourite person ever, plus some of the most
badly built palaces and tasteless monuments imaginable. No
one could fail to have seen the quality of the workmanship
in some of those palaces, it was non-existent. Small men
with big ideas that revolve around . . . their favourite subject.
Caligula, Tiberius and Nero were, in my opinion, the cam-
pest dictators of all and Rome the model on which all their
deluded despotic regimes are based – if only they hadn't
spent all the money on temples to self-deification and lavish
follies. If I look into a glass (darkly) I can see myself as a
mini Caligula. I've even been called a dictator once or twice,
so in Rome I feel at home.

•

I found myself in Rome because I was scheduled to appear as
one of the headliners (along with Grace Jones and Geri
Halliwell) at Rome's first big Gay Pride Festival, the largest it
has ever had (or at least for the past 2,000 years). There is,
exclaimed the promoter, a storm of controversy because more
than one hundred thousand gay men and women were intent
on marching through Rome, and the Pope was having a seizure
(certainly not the first by the look of him), and was condemn-
ing the march and predicting Hell and Retribution. Now I
don't want to be disrespectful to his Holiness, but seeing him
propped up and driven round in his bullet-proof Popemobile
(though admittedly it is quite fabulous) one can't help thinking, isn't it time to call it a day and send him off to retire?
Watching him deliver those sermons is painfully worrying as
you feel he could keel over and die before the Amen.

I adore Catholicism. Meekness and humility, simple values
and understatement. Not a chance! Take a stroll round the
Vatican. It is without comparison the grandest, most vulgar,
most opulent work ever undertaken by mortal man. Marble
splendour, gold ornate statues, murals beyond comparison,

decadent and extravagant, and that is just the gift shop; a place where anything and everything is available from 3D images of the saints, plastic rosaries, Pope table mats, T-shirts and Day-Glo crucifixes.

It is the Las Vegas of religions.

•

It was hellishly hot when I arrived and the hotel was just not suitable. The fact it incorporated a shopping complex bode badly, and not encouraging me was its proximity to the airport. How the hell could I lurk around the Coliseum and pose by the Trevi fountain (like Anita Ekberg in *La Dolce Vita*) when I'm located out in the middle of nowhere. No, this just won't do!

I didn't care that the promoter informed me that Grace Jones felt it suitable and was staying put. Geri, like me, wanted out, but for a quite separate reason: she apparently felt it inappropriate to be in the same hotel (or square mile) as Grace. The promoter told me all the details afterwards, though of course I can't substantiate them, only repeat them: that Geri had a verbal bout with Grace (hearsay), that Grace had a fist fight with Geri (hearsay), that Geri had demanded a white horse for her stage entrance (fact) which later shat all over the stage (the horse not Geri), and that once she was mounted on the steed it nearly bolted into the audience, taking her and her ever so shocking wedding dress attire with it (fact), that her dancers had to now contend with a slippery stage covered in horse shit, risking life and limb for their, well, let's call it art for want of a better word (fact).

Now Geri arriving on stage on a horse clearly seemed an attempt to upstage Grace's entrance (down an enormous disguised staircase), but the horse shitting and bolting suddenly meant it began to not seem such a coup, so Geri clumsily dismounted and decided to use Grace's stage prop – the staircase – to cavort around on, finally mimicking several sexual positions with one of her dancers in an attempt to shock this Catholic audience, which produced not so much as a gasp of shock but a collective yawn.

•

With the fiasco of the appearance over, I was away. As the night opened up, I climbed in the car with my guides, two Italian girls who worked for the promoter, and told them to show us the more unusual sights and places in Rome. They cast a sideward glance at each other, silently agreeing on where they should take us, mischievously smiling as they directed the driver.

A short drive later, up twisting roads, we arrived at a hillside car park that overlooked the city. Rome on a balmy summer night is breathtaking: and since words escape me, I'll move on. The thing is that when locals show you these sorts of sights, standing proudly beside you while you gasp in awe and throw in a few perfunctory questions, you never quite know how long to keep it up without offending them. They pointed out familiar landmarks, informing me that just adjacent to the car park was the site of the gladiator race-track, and beyond that you could make out the remains of what was Nero's palace.

After a short while I cautiously suggested we move on, somewhere 'special'. They explained that they had only intended this as a slight diversion on our way to a very special place.

The car drove through the cluttered streets, historical ruins and religious monuments at every turn, past statues and palaces of staggering beauty and insane vulgarity, past silhouetted villas and vibrant coffee shops. Eventually the car pulled into what appeared to be a deserted area, an expanse of openness dimly lit.

The driver turned off the engine.

'Are we here?' I enquired.

'Yes. It is a place known as the underworld,' my guide informed us. 'It is where the lost people come.'

Suddenly I could see shadowy figures approaching the car, laughing, whistling, howling; then I could see they were transvestites and transsexuals parading their wares. Several moved into the beams of the car headlights, posing seductively over the bonnet, shouting at us, all manner of strange shapes, muscular torsos in mini dresses, skinny over-made-up boys in tight catsuits, gulping from bottles and vying for attention, lifting their skirts and caressing their silicon breasts. I noticed other cars pull in or heard engines start up and head out, their attentions shifting, some moving away, others desperately coaxing us to open the car window. Like hyenas they circled our car, smudged lips pressed to the glass, enticing sirens. Dust rose as they paced the dry ground in a pack. As I strained to see, my elbow pressed on the electric window button and instantly the window went down. Everyone in the car panicked. But too late. A rough as hell creature in a blond wig lunged in at me, her mascara running down her cheeks, her Jaggeresque lips pouting, her eyes wide and crazy. A muscular tattooed arm grabbed me and pulled me towards her, trying to kiss me, while her other hand ran spider-like towards my crotch, deftly searching out my pockets. Realizing I was in no immediate danger my guides helped untangle me from her clutches, and she pulled back as the window slid shut, grabbing my gold necklace, half garrotting me, leaving an ugly raw red welt around my throat. But try as she might the chain did not break.

It was then, and to this day I still can't fathom it, that my, let's call him my 'travelling companion' did the unthinkable. He got out of the car to take a photo. Our guides panicked and shouted for him to get back in, but too late. At once several transsexuals, pushing and shoving, surrounded him, hands frisking his body. One suddenly had the camera, another pulled his coat off, while a third yanked at his watch. Suddenly I saw others in the distance sensing a kill and moving towards him as he struggled to keep his balance, to grab back his camera.

I wanted to get out to help him but was held back by our guides who shouted for him to get back in the car. Momentarily he broke free and threw himself into the car, pursued by the stubbled harpies as the door slammed shut.

The engine started up and we accelerated away, transvestites screaming at us and hitting the metalwork, one throwing herself onto the bonnet.

As we pulled out onto the main road my guides looked at me expectantly.

'They call them, how does it translate ... Without shadow. Almost not people, but ...'

She abandoned trying to translate it.

Our other guide said, 'It's hard to think of them as people, somebody's children.'

My companion said one of them had a knife, which didn't surprise me. I thought again of the film *Suddenly, Last Summer* in which Elizabeth Taylor's cousin has been set upon by a gang of Moroccan youths who then literally eat him alive (that's Tennessee Williams for you), which lends itself to a close-up of Taylor's expression of remembrance – the horror is all too clear in a wide-eyed and biting-her-knuckle way. 'Gobbling. Gobbling. Gobbling,' she describes the frenzied attack. Gobbling indeed.

But when my travelling companion was back there, out of the car, we can only imagine what might have happened to him. They were like a cock-eyed troupe of Anna Magnanis on amphetamine. I was in a state of shock while my companion thought it all just fabulous – well, he was several years younger than me, and youth is dismissive, that is until he discovered that his pockets had been picked clean.

•

I managed later that night to see a video recording of my appearance on stage, which after my ambush by the hellish hookers now seemed an age ago. Prior to my performance my companion had downed several Es, drank an entire bottle of champagne and decided to run on stage while I performed, taking off most of his clothes and bounding around in a mindless display, simulating sex and masturbation. I recall he was in my eye-line, cavorting around, but I was trying to concentrate on performing. Watching the recording of the show I now saw the full extent of how insane he was. I envisaged what was left of my Italian career, albeit not that much, go down the sink with the pasta.

Jesus H. Christ, I thought, this is a religious country, this is a Catholic city, this is after all the home of the Pope. So there I was agog in front of the monitor thinking what was he thinking when my mobile phone rang.

I answered it and a husky voice boomed out, 'Helloo-oooo, dahhhhrrrling, it's meeeee, Grace.'

'Grace?' I asked quizzically.

'Grace. *Grace Jones.*'

Oh my God, I thought, it's Grace Jones.

'Who fucking else did you think it would be?'

It was a good question. I thought maybe 'His Grace'.

'Hi, Grace,' I gushed, all fingers and thumbs. 'What is it?'

'I love you. *I love you sooo much! Darling!* And you know what I'm thinking? *We must do a song together soon.*'

'Sure, Grace, I'd love to and I love you too.' (How the hell did she get my number?)

'I will call you, when this whole *nightmare* piece of shit is over, darling. You hear me, I'll call you!'

•

It occurred to me while in Rome that my midlife crisis could be resolved if only I could find a religion, then maybe my life would be more centred and orderly. I often think about Jesus; there was a guy with a design for living, a sort of latter-day Conran, and talk about common sense.

I want to believe, really, but I keep having this problem. Basically it comes down to the fact that I just think the concept of God is nonsense. I like Christmas and I like Bette Midler, but that doesn't add up to buying this God stuff. Now far be it from me to knock anyone who's found religion, good on you I say, but don't tell me you're right and in turn I won't knock your idiotic delusional beliefs.

This Christian Evangelist rang on my door the other day – you know, those door to door ones – as I was packing for my trip to Rome and just late generally. He told me I was not happy, not fulfilled. You're in pain. And as I walked out past him I thought, he's right. But it's what's missing in my life that spurs me on, gives me the fuel – it's the pain of life that makes any pleasure more sweet.

It's not just God, it's religion too. It's actually all nonsense. And I got to thinking, how can anyone with a degree of intelligence believe that hokum, but they do, so what do I know? They say at the moment of death there are no atheists, but how the hell do they know that?

I suppose Buddhism is the most appealing but that's taken. Then maybe some Tibetan sect, but it just seems that all the best ones are spoken for.

Nobody wants the 'other ones'.

Especially not these days.

If you know what I mean.

12

To Russia with Love

'The church is close but the road is icy. The bar is far, but I will walk carefully.'

– Russian proverb

•

How did it all begin? How did I ever get myself into this? Three years in Russia, recording the most difficult album of my career? This journey, a love–hate affair, over-blown drama and bureaucratic nightmare that I embarked upon, was the turning point in my life, and came at a time when I thought I least needed it.

•

I studied my face in the mirror and saw how Russia had aged me, not only physically, but also emotionally and mentally. Russia had taken its toll – too many poor-quality meals, extreme weather: minus 35 degrees freezing winters through to 100 degrees plus blistering humid summers. I'd been in the Moscow air, thick as borsch, with choking pollution and chemical toxicity. I'd had sleepless nights and frustration macheting my way through the swathe of bureaucracy and etiquette.

But the last thing in the world I expected was that Russia would become my second home, a place where I would visit, work, and then find myself staying over for longer and longer periods, eventually spending much of my time in an apartment I acquired in Moscow.

In middle age, I found something of what I'd been missing, and I found it in Russia of all places.

•

Sometimes we agree to things because, firstly, they are so far ahead it seems less of an inconvenience.

For example, my mother might say, 'Oh, I'm coming to London next Easter for the weekend. Will you show me around?' So I agree because next Easter is like ten months away, and not something I need to worry about now. Then I forget all about it. Until suddenly one evening my mother calls saying that her train gets in at noon tomorrow and could I meet her.

The second reason you agree to do something is because you feel it will be over in a short time and, well, it might be worth doing and hell, it's only a month out of your life, and like the first reason, it's not even planned to begin till next year, so you agree.

That is how it was with the Russian album project.

Some way off (with the reality that it would probably never transpire) and only a month of my time, I committed to it.

And anyway, how does that old Russian proverb go? 'He who doesn't risk never gets to drink champagne.'

•

I had been to Russia before, ten years earlier at the beginning of the nineties, so one might say our courtship had tentatively begun. I was invited by the British Council to tour the country with a series of acoustic shows. Anyway, all this is marvellously documented in my critically acclaimed bestseller *Tainted Life* so we don't need to go into it here, but just to mention that it was while touring that a fan handed me a cassette of Russian Romance songs, including several by the singers and songwriters Alexander Vertinsky and Vadim Kozen. Enquiring what the term Russian Romance meant, I was told 'songs from the last century that were "in touch" with the Russian soul'.

Perhaps French Chanson is the nearest comparison in terms of structure and delivery. Similar songs in America or England might be considered Torch, in Portugal Fado, in Spain Flamenco – they share a common thread, speak of lives lived, passion, lost love, struggle and survival.

Listening to songs in an unfamiliar foreign language, the most one has to glean from them might be an emotional atmosphere. Maybe the vocal sound or the melody stirred you too. But it was this emotional passion that took hold of me when I first played that cassette of Romance songs, and when they were translated, their meaning made clear, they truly touched me.

•

I had already recorded albums dedicated to Jacques Brel. On first hearing I didn't understand a word he was singing but felt compelled by the passion of his delivery. Hearing Scott Walker, David Bowie and Alex Harvey sing Brel deepened my fascination with his artistry.

As far as other foreign artists' work, I have sung Chanson songs translated for me, songs by Juliette Greco, Leo Ferre, Barbara and Serge Lemain. And of course the truly great Charles Aznavour.

In turn I wrote songs in these styles for my albums *Torment* and *Toreror* and *Mother Fist*.

As I was to discover it was this body of past work that

had led Misha Kucherenko, executive producer and business-man, to approach me with the idea of recording an album of Russian Romance songs.

•

I first met Misha in 1998 when he handed me a CD he'd produced (by which I mean financed) of a woman in her nineties, a singing Romance legend called Alla Bayanova. He urged me to listen to it, suggesting I should record a song with her, and that he could make it happen. I didn't doubt his seriousness, but doubted Alla would live long enough to see it happen.

Time passed and I heard no more from Misha.

Then one day back in London towards the end of the millennium, I received a call from the St Petersburg artist Sergey Bugaev, known as Afrika. He suggested I should record a track with the St Petersburg Naval Choir.

'Imagine yourself,' he said, 'surrounded by a naval choir, singing in Russian – that would be something, wouldn't it?'

I imagined it.

It would certainly be something special. But, as I explained to him, it was a big decision, I'll have to think about, uhm, all right, I'll do it.

I know what you're thinking. Like being surrounded by seventy young Russian sailors, in their uniforms, had some-thing to do with my decision.

I can assure you that thought never even occurred to me, except when I wrote this. But thinking about it then and knowing the reality of even gaining access to a military choir, I suspected it was going to remain just a great idea.

Then I began to get calls from Misha Kucherenko again. He had spoken to the 'living legend' Alla Bayanova who had said she would like to record a song with me. Misha then suggested I should do an album of Russian Romance songs, with simple piano accompaniment, and Alla could feature as a guest on one or two of the tracks. It would take a month, Misha assured me, if that. Alla wanted to do this. A month, he repeated.

I was reticent.

But Misha was persistent.

In honesty my reticence stemmed from the reality that it looked an impossibly fanciful notion. I spoke no Russian, discovered that Alla spoke no English (and resolutely refused to) and we would be recording songs in Russian. Who would translate, who would finance it, what songs? I began to dismiss it all as unrealistic, and then began to avoid Misha's calls.

But the next thing I was to discover about Russians is that once they are in your life they are very hard to get out. And Russians with an idea and purpose are nigh on imposs-ible. So it was with Misha, who relentlessly pursued me for an answer, by any means possible, undeterred by any doubts I expressed.

Eventually I suppose he wore me down. I decided to go with it and see where it would lead. That has always been my philosophy in music, and why it has not always been about commercial output that might end up in that bewilder-ing place called the charts. After all, it is about having an interesting life, about great or not so great experiences, and producing something in the process. The hope is that out of it you might create something that others enjoy and that might lead them to listen to other people's music – those that influence you as an artist.

I called Misha and agreed to do it, providing that I lost no money of my own. I also made it clear to him that whoever was financing it must be able to afford to lose their investment – if they couldn't, then they shouldn't do it. I explained that if they were expecting every cent of their money back they were not to undertake it. I for one didn't want to be owing money to Russians. It must be a labour of love.

Misha seemed clear on this point and the project was underway.

After several trips back and forth I began recording the album in earnest in early October 2001, only a few days before the war on Afghanistan commenced. Over the following two years I would make countless trips to Russia, too numerous to recall. All you need to know is the journey is tedious, the food not worth mentioning and the arrival at Moscow airport always a nightmare.

13

Moscow and St Petersburg

Flying tip: Avoid Russian airlines whenever possible

•

When flying to Moscow always try to get a seat near to the front of the aircraft because you need to get off the plane as quickly as possible. This is because Russian passport control is chaotic. Once you reach passport control do not attempt to speak any Russian; if you are asked anything shrug and repeat 'diplomat' impatiently. Even if the passport officer doubts you they won't pursue it, just in case you are. Sure enough you'll be through to baggage claims in no time. Now you have learned the first and most important lesson about Russia and Russians – attitude is everything.

Most ordinary Russians trying to eek out an existence (and that includes the customs guards and police) are wary of crossing anyone with attitude because they don't know who you are, or more importantly don't know who you are connected to. Upsetting the wrong person in Russia can be disastrous for their well-being, and that of their family, their much-loved family pets and everyone they've ever met.

Russia is a tough place to live, and Russians are on the whole extremely poor and see you as a rich Westerner, rich enough to travel so therefore considerably wealthier than themselves, therefore fair game. I am not suggesting you will be mugged; that is not how it is done. Everything is more subtle than that. Most Russians are honest and hard-working people, but you won't meet them. Chances are you will inevitably meet dubious individuals who will slyly attempt to separate you from your hard currency at every opportunity. Stand your ground and take no nonsense.

It is also worth mentioning the officials at the airport, almost always women, always absolute bitches who make no effort to disguise their utter contempt for foreigners. They parade around in uniforms that belong in the seventies: stilettos, black stockings, split mini skirts and tight bosom-lifting tunics, their hair teased back, panstick and turquoise eyeshadow, looking for all the world like those girls I went to school with: love bites, enormous knotted ties (top button undone) and a packet of ten Embassy No 6.

Once through the rigmarole of customs you are outside trying to fight your way through the crowd of touting taxi drivers. In fact the airport is one of the few places you actually find taxi drivers. Elsewhere in the city they are redundant. If you want to go somewhere you simply stick out your hand and a car will stop, almost always ready to take you anywhere for 100 roubles. I have never had to wait more than a minute before a car screeches to a halt. As a Westerner I find it quite amazing, this degree of trust. You do of course need to speak Russian or have a local with you, or at least a note in Russian. Often a group of us will be picked up by a female driver and taken wherever we want to go, something unimaginable in the West. I find myself pondering where these people were going that they could take time out to give a lift.

To live and work in Russia, particularly Moscow, you have to be a little unhinged. It is a place in which you can take nothing for granted – even going out of the house requires planning as everything is in a constant state of chaos. Simple tasks like getting from one place to another require a strategy, for instance having to allow yourself an extra hour on your journey because the traffic is gridlocked constantly. This may account in part for the first truth about Russians – they are always late, seeming to have no concept of time-keeping. I mean really late: not minutes but hours, eventually arriving unapologetically, quite oblivious of any prior arrangements. I found this infuriating (being obsessively punctual as only the English are) but my complaints made not a jot of difference.

•

Having eventually negotiated a taxi to take you from the airport, and after much pushing and shoving, having squeezed everything you own into a Lada, you're off. The drive will be terrifying, believe me, involving high-speed reckless overtaking, sharp braking and generally being thrown around. That is until you approach central Moscow, then it will be a crawl in the traffic as carbon monoxide fumes fill the car. Winding the windows down is not an option as the window handles are always missing. Meanwhile, the radio will be turned up to full volume blaring out tinny Russian pop music whilst the driver sings along and chain-smokes.

Then without fail the car will be pulled over by the militia (police, as they're still affectionately known in other countries) and the car will be inspected until some fault is discovered, or our IDs will be scrutinized until some discrepancy is found – all usually invented. The single purpose of this is to enable them to threaten one or more of us with arrest, which of course they would rather not do if this could be settled some other way.

Hmmm – some other way!

Everyone is silent.

Again the militiaman will repeat himself, and though I

don't understand what he is saying, I clearly grasp what he wants.

It is the path of least resistance that makes rivers and men crooked.

Negotiations begin, and money is handed over and you are waved on. This annoyance happens a great deal. In one evening I have been in a car stopped no less than six times. We call it bribery but here it's a negotiable 'on the spot' fine.

In fact everything is negotiable (from your taxi to your traffic fine to your hotel room – even in the best five-star hotels). But be warned about hotels. Everything has hidden extras (hotel rooms include city tax, 'room tax' and my favourite, 'hospitality tax', whatever that is).

Everything is designed to confuse you. Most tourist restaurants or hotels price everything in units (roughly meaning dollars or euros) but make you pay the equivalent in roubles, as it is now illegal for establishments to take foreign currency as payment, so hotels but also some restaurants have their own 'currency exchange facility' and how much is a unit? Whatever they want it to be.

Everything is paradoxically cheap and expensive. The rule is the lowest quality at the highest price. Or if something is good quality forget it, you can't afford it.

Generally everything is too much trouble. Waiters, receptionists, doormen, taxi drivers, most people in the service industry just can't be bothered. Waitresses stand around bored or chatting, making no attempt to serve customers, and when they do eventually slouch over they look at you like you're a steamy fresh dog turd. And when they realize you can't even speak Russian they tut, roll their eyes and slouch off to get an English menu, which they return with and throw at you. Then you are faced with the task of making sense of the translations which suggest nothing of what is on offer.

'Meat in sauce'
'Pigs Face in soup'
'Cock Combs'
'Brain Pie'
'Chicken Feet'

Where the hell are the rest of the animals?

Eventually the meal is slammed down in front of you, and no matter what you ordered it always looks like that chicken stock your mother made when she boiled the carcass for six hours. It is rumoured there are great restaurants serving good food at reasonable prices, but in my countless visits I've rarely found them.

Moscow, like most of Russia, is in a mess, but it still astounds me.

The views can be awe-inspiring and the architecture breath-taking, yet a few metres later it can be grotesque and tasteless. Modern Moscow has more casinos per square mile than any-where else in the world, and more spring up every month, whole buildings covered in the most garish neon and flashing lights imaginable. A more cynical person might suggest casi-nos have something to do with money laundering, but far be it for me to suggest such a thing. My favourite description of Moscow and one that sums it up to perfection is simply, 'Moscow is like Ancient Rome run by Blackpool Council.'

And it really is.

Free advice: *Don't go to a Russian casino.*

If you feel the urge to go then I suggest you decide how much you are prepared to lose, and just hand it over at the door without going in. This will save time and frustration. If you decide against my advice and gamble, *you will lose.*

The city is dominated by seven enormous Soviet build-ings, almost phantasmagorical in design, behemoths that plunge upwards, each topped with a red star. They were

Stalin's legacy (some of his better ones I might add). It is rumoured his plan was to have beams of light from one to the next, and when viewed from the air they would create an enormous star of light the length and breadth of Moscow – but if the stories are to be believed someone miscalculated and set them too far apart (breaking that bad news to Stalin can't have been easy) which if not true is quite plausible. Hitler too had wanted to create such a spectacle of light in the shape of a swastika. I ask you, what a pair they were. Imagine if they'd got together and ruled the world what a nightmare hell of sinister kitsch swastikas and stars would have lit the night sky.

•

Misha arranged a meeting with Alla Bayanova at her apartment, though it quickly became apparent to me that I was auditioning for her. Alla wasn't a fan of the English language; in fact I discovered she hated the sound of it, refusing to even attempt it. She preferred Russian or her native Romanian. Within moments of meeting me, she made it clear that she held deep misgivings as to whether I was even capable of singing Russian Romance songs at all. I was in agreement with her on that at least.

I sat nervously in Alla's apartment as she looked me up and down. All I could think was, be glad you had this moment.

It was a typical Moscow apartment block: a dark, concrete structure. Inside, long corridors ran the length of the building, punctuated by reinforced doors (no doubt to keep the militia out).

Yet inside the apartment it was cosy, decorated in typical Eastern European style. Dark wood furnishings, wall carpets, and an assortment of pictures and photos, from floor to ceiling, all depicting Alla throughout her eighty-year career – film stills, record covers, framed pictures of herself posing with other stars and politicians, and of course family photos. She was very beautiful in her youth and even now, in her late nineties, something shone through.

Don't cry because it's over, smile because it happened

•

Alla reclined back off her crutches and into her chair, carefully balancing the crutches on the floor (they assisted her walking after a recent hip-replacement operation). She was smaller than I imagined, and I guessed her apparent fragility was as much age as illness. Heavily made up with large owlish glasses, she retained an air of girlishness and mischief.

She chatted to my interpreter while intently studying me, commenting that I was handsome but why did I have gold teeth, which she thought to be horrible.

Other family members joined us and served tea and Alla put a record onto the old gramophone and began to sing along to the music, encouraging me to join her. Now obviously not knowing the words, I 'la-la-la' along, and harmonized when I could. Before you know it we're singing in unison, sort of. The Russian legend and the British artist Marc Almond – it works for me. Misha was delighted because it seemed I had passed the audition.

We sipped tea and decided to record two quite simple songs, which I was to record in Russian, and use her piano player, both at her insistence.

A couple of months later I watched Alla as she took a workshop held in Moscow in front of maybe two hundred people. She was giving instructions and criticisms to a selection of

young singers who desired to sing Romance. Alla sat on the
stage while each singer took it in turn to perform. At any
moment Alla would hold up her hand, stop the performer
and chat about how they might improve their delivery or
technique, in turn leading by example and singing, thereby
teaching and entertaining at the same time. She was undoubtedly the master of Romance songs and, along with the audience, these protégés, heads bowed in respect, hung on her
every word.

To have the chance to work with Alla Bayanova was
extremely important for me, as it endorsed what I was doing
with true authenticity. And not just that, but Alla is a real piece
of musical history, has lived such a fantastic impossible terrible life that when she passes a tie with the past will be cut.

•

Misha had made a CD of songs that he thought I would
like, and listening to them we eventually narrowed it down
to fifteen or so songs.

Over the successive months I came to know Misha and
count him as a friend, so I want to take the time to tell you
about him.

Misha Kucherenko is an incredible man, and without him
the Russian album would not have happened. He revealed
to me in the course of the years we spent together so much
about Russia and Russian people.

Now in his late thirties he was born in eastern Russia, his
parents both engineers, a child of the Communist era and the
archetypal state family, who believed utterly in their country
and its politics. He qualified as a nuclear physicist, an exem-
plary member of the state party, his future mapped out.

But Russia, like Misha, was unstable, felt outside of the
world, unable to adjust to change and reluctant to let go of
the past.

Misha had doubts about his sexuality, doubts which were to consume him. He succumbed to psychiatric treatment. The state incarcerated him and subjected him to six years of realignment therapy.

It, of course, never worked, leading only to deep depression.

With the fall of the Iron Curtain and perestroika, Misha accepted what he was, and began a new life. But talking with him about the past I sensed a feeling of disappointment and betrayal. He truly believed, and still does, that the old Communist state was a glorious achievement. He staunchly defends much of what it represented and he has a sadness and bitterness about what Russia has become. But ironically Misha has adapted more than any other Russian I have met, finding a firm place in the new Russia.

When I sit with him, what strikes me the most, other than his towering height and bulk, is his absolute unswerving belief that the West is to blame for many of Russia's problems and especially their current economic crisis. His views are at best eccentric (though resonate some truth), and at worst preposterous. His belief that America may fire nuclear weapons at Moscow any time soon, or that the Americans were responsible for 9/11 themselves (no, literally), and that Bin Laden was in cahoots with George Bush about it, go a long way in revealing something of the Russian psyche.

He refutes anything contrary to these beliefs with notions of conspiracy theories and anti-Russian propaganda. And one discovers very quickly that he will not be convinced otherwise. Nor will many Russians.

But that is the way Russians are. Under communism and state rule, Misha as a child was not given access to the truth, or shall we say alternative opinions. He was indoctrinated with mistrust of the West and cannot rid himself of it, even in the face of evidential truth.

And that is why I adore him.

But Misha is paradoxically a successful businessman and travels the world, spending a great deal of time in the US (which he condemns) but is quite happy to do business with (claiming he is exploiting the capitalists in doing so).

On a lighter note, I just want to say Misha is a complete and utter eccentric. Naturally he would refute this as true eccentrics would, but nevertheless it is true. For example, his clothes and glasses are always, without exception, coordinated by style and colour. He rarely sleeps, spending every night in one particular club at his own table, drinking tea and conducting his business affairs on no less than three mobile phones that ring continually. He eats only soup and desserts, smokes preposterously huge Cuban cigars and writes everything down in notebooks in a minute illegible scrawl, carefully indexing each entry with coloured stickers.

Yet he considers himself quite normal, unaware that the rest of the world does not live like this.

But Misha charmed me. He had a plan and was determined to make this album. He is well connected and highly respected in Moscow and St Petersburg, had the financial backing and the conviction. Above all else, he had a vision. I was going along for the ride.

•

So that first tentative step had been taken. A simple piano album of songs, with two of the tracks featuring Alla Bayanova.

Misha suggested we needed to spend some time in St Petersburg in order to make some vital contacts to ensure the album will be as good as it can be.

•

St Petersburg is totally different from Moscow; in fact it is unlike anywhere else on earth. It is a beautiful decaying monument of grand folly and design, right down to its very location.

St Petersburg was built on the backs of slaves. None of the materials required for its construction is to be found anywhere in the natural environment of the city. The story is told of workers from the countryside bearing loads of dirt on their pummelled backs (there being no solid earth on which to build in St Petersburg itself) and then being buried in the ground they carried as they died from exhaustion. Hundreds of thousands are supposed to have perished during the raising of the city. Floods, fires, disease, scurvy and packs of wolves added to the threat.

In fact so many people died creating it that St Petersburg is still referred to darkly among Russians as a city 'built on bones'. Russians regard it as an unlucky place – men and women of the heartland, that is, whom St Petersburg's own residents dismiss as provincial fools and malcontents.

It is connected to Moscow by a single straight road except for a slight indent in the centre where it is said the pencil skirted Stalin's finger as he held down the ruler when marking out the design. Such was the fear he instilled that they followed his blueprint to the finest detail. This road is known as the road of death, built on the bones of thousands of victims of Stalin's regime. But rumours and hearsay are part of Russian life, as is death, which is everywhere, especially during the last century. A Russian told me that 'Russians always feel close to death'.

In St Petersburg one senses much more than anywhere else in Russia a feeling of past suffering and struggle, but also a sense of activism and separatism and hope. As Russians like to say, 'Even in the most desolate wilderness, the stars shine brightest in the clearest sky.'

•

The day after we arrived in St Petersburg the war against Afghanistan by the US-led forces began. Many Russians I spoke to were incensed that America had attacked Afghanistan (which struck me as a bit rich since Russia spent eight years attacking it) and were convinced that the US were only interested in global domination and oil. But isn't everyone interested in oil (and global domination if they could get away with it)? And few countries more so than Russia. Still their distrust and hatred of America are deeply embedded.

Now since I was Western and Britain is an ally of America, it was let's blame Marc. It seems even with young Russians, that old Soviet indoctrination is still there – part pride, part anger, mostly frustration and resentment. My friend Natasha said, 'Bitterness runs through Russians like words through candy rock – you can never get rid of it.'

In St Petersburg we met up with songwriter and musician Boris Grebeshnikov, who Misha informed me would be contributing to the album. Though delighted, I was suddenly seeing this project opening up somewhat. Boris is the godfather of Russian contemporary music. He was one of the first to start breaking down barriers. When he first performed with the band Aquarium in the early seventies he was immediately arrested. His music was not considered 'state friendly' – it was subversive and dangerous (meaning critical) and Boris was labelled a dissident.

At that time there was only the state-run record label, which released all recordings, but did pay royalties. All lyrics had to be submitted to the Ministry of Communication for approval for clearance (Ministry of Lyrics). I discovered when searching through a swathe of songs translated for this album project how many dealt with menial issues in their lyrics – letters at the post office, lost jewellery, walking in the forest – which was a direct result of the level of censorship incurred.

I chose one of his songs for the album, entitled 'Gosur-danyia' (which translates as 'Mother Russia' or 'Your Majesty'). His group Aquarium provided the backing. We went to his studio, set in an artist complex off Nevsky Prospekt. It was adorned with little religious artefacts, icons, Buddhist statues, Easter temples and burning incense. It was filled with peace and tranquillity.

Boris told me of his special love of St Petersburg, how it is the art, and Moscow is the state, and never the two can meet.

•

The album was now diversifying and, as I was to discover, Misha had many, many more ideas of where he could take this album.

'It needs to span the century, to be a history of Russian Romance,' said Misha, sucking on an infuriating cigar, 'from the late 1900s to the present day.'

His cellphone rang.

'Oh, excuse me, Marc. *Priviat!*'

His second cellphone now rang. He picked it up.

'Could you hold on, one minute. *Priviat.* I have to call you back.'

He hung up, cupped his hand over the other cellphone and leaned over to me.

'I have Sergey Penkin on the phone – he wants to record a song with you. He is on his way over now. Will that be OK?'

I nodded resignedly.

•

It seemed over the course of the next few months Misha became completely carried away. The project was getting bigger and more people were coming on board, which made it become more complicated and stressful. Every other day there seemed to be a new meeting with someone else interested in working on the project, another collaboration.

I left Misha to his networking and met up with someone from years earlier called Vladik Mamyshev-Monroe, a talented and famous artist in Russia and the first drag queen on Russian television (for which he was incarcerated in an asylum). Over the years he has exhibited all over Russia; his most famous work was a thirty-foot self-portrait of Adolf Hitler in Red Square.

I met up with Vladik and my friend Sergey Afrika (accompanied by his permanent cameraman) to be taken around the Hermitage Museum where we posed among the rooms of golden coaches and outrageous collections of art (over 2 million pieces) – so much art that they have barely the room to store it. Literally chock-a-block with old masters to rival Amsterdam's Rijksmuseum or the Vatican, not to mention a stash of Impressionists that would be the envy of the Musée d'Orsay in Paris.

Formidable old women sat guarding each room, barking out warnings, waving frantically if you walked the wrong way, moved too near the artwork or lingered to study a painting or sculpture. Lingering in front of the art is positively discouraged.

Art overdose point came very quickly as there is only so much art you can take in, and the eleven miles of corridors packed with it would find even Brian Sewell struggling with his superlatives.

It is worth noting that museums in Russia have an unofficial two-tier entry price: a lower price for Russians and a much higher price for foreigners (so go with a Russian and keep quiet).

In order to counter all this beauty overload, we made our way across the river to Peter the Great's Museum of Anthro-

КАФЕСАД НОВЫЙ ГОД
в традиционном русском стиле

АЛЛА БАЯНОВА · MARC ALMOND

Above: Summer 2003, Dacha with Misha and Sergey, enough said.
Below left: St Petersburg, 2003. Below right: Moscow 2003.

Сандуновские бани

St Denis steam baths, Moscow.

Mark and Sergey Ignatov outside
Sinners club St Petersburg.

With the Russian naval choir, St Petersburg.

САЛОН КРАСОТЫ
СЕРГЕЙ ЗВЕРЕВ
&
КВЕЛИ
418-8092, 418-8428
Барвиха, 72

Sergey Sverev, Russia's
flamboyant top hairdresser.

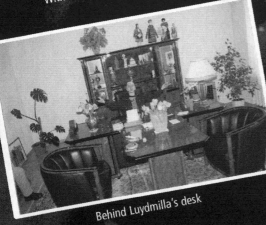

Behind Luydmilla's desk

'Russia Remember Yourself'

Luydmilla signs an autograph.

Singing with Alla Bayanova.

Rehearsing with Alla.

Photos: © Misha Kucherenko and Sergey Ignatou.

Alla's star of fame.

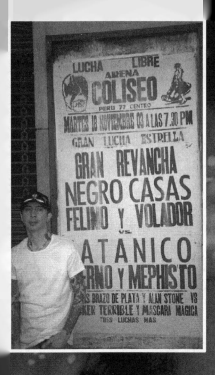

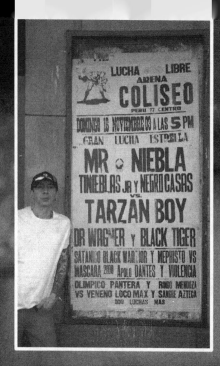

Above: Mexican wrestling posters.

Opposite middle: At the pyramid of the sun, Mexico, 2003.

Opposite bottom: With my new band at Garibaldi Square, Mexico City, 2003.

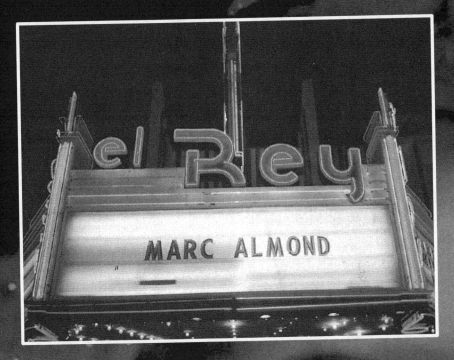

Top: A name in lights. Above: In LA, 2002.
Opposite: Just another day out with
some geeza-birds.

The author today. Photo: © Jamie McLeod.

pology and Ethnography, or Kunstkammer, with its creepy collection of genetic freaks in jars, foetuses and still-born infants, conjoined creatures, multiple limbs protruding from unnatural regions, all manner of human disfigurement floating in jars, unseeing eyes, frozen in the thick fluid, gazed upon by the curious.

Was this what Peter the Great would lovingly spend an evening in browsing? A collection of freaks and misfits? Sort of eighteenth-century Channel Five.

And on to the Geological Museum, which houses a map of the Soviet Union that's over twenty-five metres long and made entirely of precious gems, including amethysts, diamonds and rubies, but the more precious gems have disappeared of late. And the Sigmund Freud Museum of Dreams, which if you're a stoner or a junkie, is a great place to while away an afternoon.

And last and probably least, the Zoology Museum to see their pièce de résistance, a Siberian woolly mammoth preserved frozen in ice. I can't tell you how excited I was at the prospect, and how saddened by the actual specimen – it looked like something knocked up out of papier mâché and a couple of wet sheepskin rugs.

We set off walking around the city, stopping at the Church of the Saviour of the Spilled Blood to give it its rather catchy full title. This marvellous Old Russian-style church was built on the spot where Emperor Alexander II was assassinated in 1881, his spilled bloodstain, a sort of questionable rusty smudge mark, roped off from visitors.

One great place to visit is the Yussoupov Palace on the Moika, the scene of the Siberian *mouzhik* Grigori Rasputin's death in 1916, which is now a museum.

In the tiny basement where Prince Felix Yussoupov claimed to have poisoned, then shot, then bludgeoned and finally taken out and drowned Rasputin, they have created a wax figure of him sitting calmly at a table and reaching for a piece of arsenic-coated candy. Russians get genuinely spooked by the look in his eyes.

Of course there isn't any evidence that Rasputin was killed this way or that it took so many methods to eventually kill him, but Russians believe it anyway. If a story is recounted enough it becomes true in Russia.

•

St Petersburg is the most magical and mythical place and I find it inspirational. I loved it from my first visit. I remember scribbling in my notebook within minutes of arrival a short line: 'City of decaying dreams, where under pink skies gold spires gleam.'

The streets are filled with drunken sailors, or once proud soldiers bolstering their income in other ways. The city has a strange sunlight and snow that sparkles like the tsar's diamonds.

I recall a photo taken of Vladik Monroe in St Petersburg that he had given me. In the black and white photo he is dressed as Marilyn Monroe, in a hand-coloured red dress and blond wig, standing on the bank of the River Neva, his arms outstretched, reaching towards freedom – a sorrowful plea, a yearning. Yet he remains grounded, lost, hopelessly faded, an American icon imprisoned and isolated in a hostile place.

I love to look at the statue of Peter the Great, whose iron features now gaze down from Lenin's perch in Moscow Station. The emperor's face has a defiant, impatient, out of control look, true-to-life qualities for a ruler who cut off the beards of his boyars, tortured his son to death and forced the terrified members of his court and retinue to smoke tobacco and drink his health with litre shots of vodka.

If you walk the length of Nevsky Prospekt, from the Alexander Nevsky Monastery at the far (unfashionable) end to Palace Square, the Admiralty and the Neva at the other, you'll get a good idea of the scale of the place.

The monument to Catherine the Great outside the Pushkin Theatre in Ostrovsky Square is the only one in the city. It's also the gay cruising ground and jokes about the empress's predilection for stallions are reinforced down the street, at the Anichkov Bridge, where four nude youths, exquisitely proportioned and cast in bronze, are dragging horses to the ground, literally, their legs and torsos bursting with the strain, the folds of their cloaks draped in such a way as to cover (barely) their doubtless enormous genitalia. It's odd that you see an artistic rendering in Russia so overtly erotic as this. When the statues were first erected in the nineteenth-century, the Emperor Nicholas I kept giving them away, first to the King of Prussia then to the King of Naples. But he couldn't get rid of them: they were always recast and erected once more.

Nothing you've read or heard about this city prepares you for its determination to be colossal and great – the acres and mountains of granite and marble; the arrow-straight lines of the roads; the soaring facades of the Rossi palaces built in exact alignment with the width of the streets; the combination, finally, of elegance and submission, of beauty and an iron fist.

Everywhere you look you see columns and arches, pilasters and domes, bridges, embankments, cathedrals and spires. The buildings appear to be gliding, while anchored in the ground.

It possesses one indubitable quality: it transforms passers-by into shadows.

It has inspired all Russia's greatest writers – Pushkin, Gogol, Dostoyevsky, even Tolstoy, owe St Petersburg a debt of inspiration. It's alive in the literary sense. It's the leading character on its own stage.

But walking around it is shocking to see degradation of most of St Petersburg's palaces and buildings: the crumbling plaster and holes in the walls, the cheap, battered floors, the proliferation of cheap building work and shoddy renovation. A consequence of poverty and extreme weather conditions every winter make it almost impossible to maintain any form of upkeep.

Looking on the bright side, you see scaffolding everywhere you go in St Petersburg. Renovation is well underway, and there's no reason to think that the city, given time and money and no revolutions, can't be restored to its former splendour, though corruption remains an obstacle as funds keep mysteriously disappearing. The bunting tin seems to be the only fund that remains untouched.

Sex is an essential form of barter in any country under stress, and Aids isn't linked specifically in Russian minds with homosexuality, since the actual practice of same-sex relations is something most Russians can't bring themselves to imagine, let alone discuss. But gay bars are abundant in St Petersburg, a thriving nightlife far outnumbering any bars or clubs in Moscow.

•

Another singer, Sergey Penkin, agreed to collaborate on a track. A household name in Russia, and now in his early forties, he was known for his dexterous vocal range, and his outrageous outfits and questionable sexuality. All sorts of rumours circulated about him, but he would neither confirm nor deny any of them.

Penkin was flown from Moscow to St Petersburg to record his vocals for the track, a song already in his repertoire called 'Strange Feelings'. He demanded first-class flights, a five-star hotel in the penthouse suite, a white Rolls-Royce at his disposal and all manner of demands, including an envelope of dollar bills, as a condition of coming. He was a man after my own heart.

The track turned out far better than I had dared to imagine, his vocals possessing a purity and pitch unlike any I have heard. He is a generous big-hearted man when sober, and a terror when drunk on vodka, but always entertaining, the centre of attention wherever he goes.

I have on several occasions seen him perform his casino show. As I pointed out, Moscow is full of casinos, and as part of the entertainment they present a dinner and cabaret and Sergey Penkin is always a popular choice. I suspect these shows are his main source of revenue, and he told me he can often do four different casinos in one evening; basically he could do them in his sleep. Lasting a gruelling forty minutes and backed by an aged rock band, he goes through a repertoire that ranges from the bizarre to the downright surreal, covering songs such as Queen's 'Who Wants To Live Forever' (struggling with the English language) through to 'Bessame Mucho', and his pièce de résistance, a fifteen-minute version of 'Feelings', during which he performs vocal acrobatics, switching from opera to scat to disco jazz (like the button selection on a Bontempi).

It's kitsch, it's truly surreal, it's a crowd-pleaser, but most of all, and I suspect something that is lost on the Russian crowd, it's ironic and Sergey knows that.

•

Over the years I have seen many casino shows in Russia, but one in particular stands out in my memory. Forget your preconceptions of what constitutes a show or entertainment because in Russia anything can pass as it.

With this in mind I went to see a Hairdressing Show held by Russia's most famous hairdresser Sergey Sverev, who commands $1500 for a cut and rinse. His appearance is androgynously striking, with unnaturally high cheekbones and even more unnaturally full lips, he is attired in flamboyant eighties clothes, and a coiffured flicked-back fringe.

When the show eventually got underway, running late like everything in Russia does, it involved several models posing on a catwalk whilst Sergey moved from one to the next, psychotically clipping their hair, thereby creating bizarre geometric styles. Meanwhile, dancers cavorted around him to blaring disco music, strobe lights flashed and the occasional pyroflash exploded.

Having finished snipping and trimming up countless barnet fairs in record time he then leaped into the audience, grabbed a woman (who I later discovered was his wife – yes, his wife) and proceeded to perform an erotic dance with her before finally taking a bow and doing a lap of honour around the tables.

Everyone applauded wildly, as though having just witnessed something extraordinary. I wondered if I had missed something and tried to recall if I'd gone to the toilet. I looked around at the audience and noticed a woman tearfully overcome by the epiphany she had just witnessed.

He was quite the emperor of hairdressing, and he had quite a suit of clothes.

I discovered afterwards that he intends to launch himself as a pop singer and plans to cover my song 'A Lover Spurned', which was a big hit in Russia. What is it with people wanting to be pop stars? Why don't people just stick to what they are good at and thank their lucky stars they have something . . . says me, trying to write a book.

•

By this time the album was well underway, and I found myself with little time to dwell on midlife and my apparent crisis. It seemed that making the album and spending so much time in Russia was therapeutic. This was what was needed: new experiences, not retreating to old ones in some vague hope of reviving the past.

Misha Kucherenko was out of control by this stage, suggesting almost on a daily basis other Russian artists who would like to collaborate. He played me various tapes of singers and groups, encouraging me to consider them, but it seemed to me we had enough already. It also became apparent that Misha was losing the plot, suggesting a variety of terrible groups who had nothing to offer other than a modicum of success in Russia.

Then I began to suspect Misha was concerned that the album, though still a way from completion, was at least on track to be finished. That day loomed as far as Misha was concerned like a dark rain cloud, ominous and foreboding. I didn't know this at the time but Misha didn't want the album to finish, ever. That was something I was to discover about Russians, their inability to draw a line under something, to let go, to call it a day.

It is not a conscious thing, but it is a fact. Russia seems to be a country where permanence is paramount; it is, after all, a country where plastic flowers are much more prized and valued than real ones.

Of all the artists Misha suggested, I agreed to one more collaboration, and that was with the singer Ilya Leguntenko, the charismatic frontman with the famous Russian group Mummi Troll. They were one of the most popular and influential groups of the last decade in Russia. Ilya was a fan of Romance music and particularly the writer Vadim Kozen, an artist who was exiled to Siberia in the middle of the last century for his homosexuality and whose plight was particularly sad.

Ilya suggested the Kozen song 'Your Affectionate Smile Has Disappeared' for us to cover. I agreed. We recorded the track and I decided the album was complete. It had been a long journey of discovery and I had arrived at a place I felt comfortable with.

•

It was New Year's Eve and I was back in Moscow to put the final touches to the album, and make several club appearances throughout the night. I want to take you through the evening ahead because it really does exemplify what Russia is like, and how insane it can be. My agent and promoter had booked me to appear at three different venues, all quite varied, in which I agreed to perform a short PA (which means live vocal to recorded backing track) of my best-known songs. The money was good too and, let's face it, what else would I be doing?

Arriving in Moscow the temperature was minus 30 degrees, which was I'm assured, quite normal for the time of year, but still extremely painful. However, there is something about Moscow covered in snow when it all seems to make sense: wrapped in a huge coat and donning a Russian hat, the snow lightly falling, blanketing everything, standing in Red Square, I felt it was quite magical.

We then headed towards the first show of the night, which commenced just after midnight. The audience were made up of ordinary Russians out for a good time, no pretensions, a chicken-in-the-basket crowd.

I want to jump ahead now to the last appearance at a club called Zeppelin, and it was four in the morning, and I was flagging a bit but it's now the home run. It was a good crowd, rowdy and drunk by this stage but enthusiastic, and a few fans had got in so that helped. It went down great, and the atmosphere spurred me on, especially after what happened earlier.

By this I mean the second show of the night. Thinking,

after the relative ease of the first show, this is easy, was I in
for a shock. That appearance was in Moscow's most expensive restaurant, and most exclusive, by which I mean there
were only about eight couples sitting eating. Firstly, I would
like to point out the food on display was obscene: buckets
of caviar, piles of lobsters, rare delicacies you can only
hazard a guess at, and bottles of vintage Dom Perignon half
drunk and scattered around. Decadence gone mad. The
men smoked Cuban cigars and looked for all the world like
characters from a Tarantino film. The women were stun-
ningly beautiful, anorexic girls toying with their salads.
They looked bored and jaded, and I sensed nothing would
entertain them. Then the promoter informed me that I was
booked to play for fifty minutes. This lot looked like they
wouldn't want more than fifty seconds of me, but the
promoter explained how we wouldn't want to upset the
host. Apparently we wouldn't like to see him upset.

Fifty minutes it would be then.

My warm-up act was a Father Christmas, immaculately
dressed in a traditional outfit trying to liven up the evening,
handing out Tiffany boxes and 'ho ho hoeing', as if his life
depended on it; and it probably did. He was accompanied
by several dancing elves.

I waited in the hall until announced. The backing track
began, the sound, of course, not working, the microphone
feeding back and the audience politely casting barely a glance
in my direction.

It seemed like a mountain to climb. By the third song I'd
run out of steam. The anorexic girlfriends started to chat to
each other, eyeing me occasionally, gormlessly pushing a
single pea around their plates. Now everyone was chatting
as I started the next song and what I sensed was happening
was that I was becoming an irritant, expecting at any
moment a gun to be produced to shoot the fucking singer.

Seeing I was dying a death the Santa and elves came on to try to liven it up. Then surreptitiously the manager, seeing my distress, sidled over and told me if I did a request for his girlfriend then we were free to go. I agreed.

The song requested was 'A Lover Spurned', which everyone failed to notice I'd already sung ten minutes earlier. The manager grabbed me and stood me in front of our host and his girlfriend and I serenaded her, feeling every bit the old crooner. I swear she'd have blushed if she'd known how. I finished and hurried out, passing a magician and a gypsy with a real-life dancing bear waiting their turn to go in and perform for the emperors and their concubines in the vomitarium. The sight of the bear dressed up in a sparkly outfit, chained and muzzled, was very sad, but I patted it on the head and whispered in its ear: 'Good luck, kid, they're a tough crowd tonight!'

•

The completion of the album meant a chance to celebrate. In Russia the slightest thing can be an excuse to celebrate. What else for it but a tour of Moscow's sleazier clubs? Firstly we visit Chance. This is its second incarnation, now a regular disco. The old club was famous as it featured young men swimming naked in a giant aquarium behind the bar. Nothing so risqué here.

One club, Three Monkeys, escaped relocation to the suburbs (like Chance), though it has moved several times but only within a short distance, and despite all the odds has survived. It is a gay club. It is unusual in Moscow for a club to allow itself such clear labelling. It's for Russians and I have seen very few foreigners there, and even fewer Westerners. One night weekly they have a wrestling competition in which Russian soldiers have to tear each other's clothes off round by round, refereed by a Jim Broadbent type, and assisted by a geisha drag queen who holds up the round number cards. If the action is a little slow the geisha will cut the wrestlers' pant elastics with a giant pair of scissors. The winner (inevitably picked earlier) gets to spend time at the club owner's table – and if that's not a euphemism then show me a bucket and spade.

Misha Kucherenko is the most infamous patron of this establishment and had his own table overlooking the proceedings where he conducted business on his mobile phone, chomping on his cigar to the annoyance of those sitting nearby, and dismissing the wrestling entertainment as 'exploitation for capitalist pigs'. Though I pointed out that as the place was full only of other Russians, and it certainly wasn't laid on for us, how could that be?

Misha refused to accept that.

Three Monkeys is a hot bed of intrigue and gossip with a regular cast of characters, mostly hustlers, playing the central roles. The club all but lost its licence recently because of a spate of murders: a customer was found skinned and beheaded, and another found stabbed and garrotted. We have since been assured that the culprits have been arrested (well, someone has anyway) and a CCTV camera has been installed at the club entrance, so everyone can feel much safer.

Anyway, we were celebrating and Misha met us at his regular table, and within an hour the cast list was over twenty-five people vying for space and drinking our health.

•

A couple of months into recording, and several more visits back and forth from London, staying at the Kempinski Hotel in Moscow was proving too expensive. I decided the only course of action was to find my own apartment.

A friend came up with a great place: three bedrooms, fairly central and not too expensive. OK, the area wasn't great, a tram rattled down the road outside from the early hours, there were a few dodgy types loitering around outside, not to mention the alcoholics in the children's playground opposite (the children themselves I'm talking about), the lift was temperamental, and arriving back late at night you might be confronted by an oversized rat in the hall but, hell, it wasn't that different from London, and it was a fraction of the cost of a hotel.

Having an apartment also meant you could eat in, saving money and more importantly avoiding life-threatening food poisoning in restaurants.

On the occasions that I do eat out I more often than not choose the restaurant Pushkin's, a famous eatery off Pushkin Square. Three floors offer a variety of cuisines in an opulent and grand atmosphere of old decadent Russia, all with a traditional Russian flair: thick soups, *pirozhky* (delicious little pies with various fillings), blinis and caviar, dumplings and strange meat and tinned fruit contrivances you would imagine couldn't work together – and usually don't. The food is good by Russian standards, so naturally it's overpriced, but riskless. The maître d' is obsessive and quirky, the staff informed and meticulously finicky. As a regular I am always whisked to the best table and pampered, even when I order little, sometimes maybe only tea. It is open twenty-four hours a day and never takes bookings, so it's a great place to go after a night out.

•

Another favourite pastime: forget the gym – Russians like to de-stress in a *banya*: a furnace-hot steam room in which they beat themselves and their friends with bundles of birch branches.

Before entering, buy a *venik* (leafy bunch of birch twigs). Start with the dry sauna (about 200°F), then go to the steam room (*parilka*) where water and eucalyptus oil are regularly ladled on to heated rocks to create steam. Now, to drive out all the toxins, dip your *venik* into a bucket of hot water to soften them a bit and flail yourself (and others). After five minutes, or longer if you can stand it, which I can't, you escape and fling yourself into the cold pool. Then, tea and blinis.

•

And finally there is Gorki Park.

It is an amusement park; well, it amuses me no end. It really should be on a DON'T GO list but I couldn't resist it. Without exception it is the worst amusement park in the world, and a poignant symbol of Russia. This once great park is now full of broken rides and abandoned attractions. There is the actual Russian space shuttle, which you can board, take a ride, and watch a film of the actual launch when Russia was a contender. I say ride but I use the word liberally – the seats sway around on hydraulics (if they are working at all) in a pitiful attempt to recreate a feeling of weightlessness, while disco lights flash and dry ice fills the cabin. It all fails so dismally, especially when the film reveals its one flight into space was unmanned.

•

Back to the Russian album. Misha continued to organize collaborations, the next being with the Russian queen of song Luydmilla Zukena. Having been told how famous she was and her standing in Russia, it seemed unlikely she would even consider it. To many older Russians who spent a lifetime listening to her on state radio she was an icon. She was a favourite of past presidents, especially Krushchev who, it is said, during a performance threw her the diamonds and jewellery that once belonged to Tsar Nicholas.

I was told she has kept prime ministers waiting outside her dressing room for hours, before eventually relenting and granting them an audience. It is also rumoured that she has unlimited access to the corridors of power in the Kremlin, and has been known to burst into Putin's office unannounced to ensure her views are heard at the highest level. Whether there is any truth to these stories is almost irrelevant – she commands such an air of authority and status that they are part of her myth. She granted the Beatles an audience at the height of their fame, and has toured the world performing to faithful Russian emigrants in every country. It is said she has wealth and properties across Russia. In Moscow she lives on the highest floor of a monstrous Gothic building (one of the seven created by Stalin), the view unparalleled in Moscow.

Luydmilla is a formidable woman, and one can be forgiven for forgetting that above all else she is an artist, a singer whose voice is unique, extraordinary and heartbreaking in its purity. Backed by her own orchestra, her voice is for me the embodiment of Mother Russia, the soul and the heart of the state.

And for many decades she was exactly that. But times changed and with the fall of the Iron Curtain and the end of Communism, she came to represent a past many Russians wanted to forget. As a party faithful member representing the old regime, she found new Russia a confusing and disrespectful place.

But all this history of her was told to me before I met her. Naturally I was terrified. A meeting had been set up after which she would decide if she wanted to collaborate with me. So nervously we made our way to her studio and headquarters to meet this living legend.

I was shown to her office and sat waiting for her in front of an enormous desk adorned with personal artefacts. A glass cabinet across the furthest wall contained a lifetime's collection of memories – photos of Luydmilla with people who I guess were Russian dignitaries or famous artists, Lalique glass vases, ornate gold crucifixes, medals and a set of intricately carved Matrashki dolls.

Suddenly the door opened and in she came, surrounded by several people fluttering around her. I stood and we were introduced. Far smaller than her legend portrays her, heavily made up and jet black hair tied back in a bun, she talked rapidly in Russian. Misha Kucherenko, plainly in awe of her, struggled to keep up translating, his gaze fixed intently on her. She was immediately concerned how thin I was and ordered soup for me, barking out a command.

We exchanged pleasantries, and I gradually relaxed a little. I found myself comparing her to Alla Bayanova. Luydmilla was the voice of the regime, whereas Alla was a victim of it – their lives worlds apart.

I told Luydmilla that in order to meet her I had forfeited my chance to meet the Queen of England, whose jubilee reception at the ICA I was invited to. The reality was that I wouldn't have actually met her, but at least been in the same room – though I neglected to point this out to Luydmilla.

On hearing that I had preferred to spend time with her over the Queen she was overjoyed, gave me a crushing hug, kissing me repeatedly, and announced that she would sing with me. I discovered she had already decided which song and that for the climax she would sing in English, something despite her long and illustrious career she had never attempted before. Excitedly she explained that we would record it immediately with her orchestra who had been rehearsing it for weeks. I began to suspect her decision to collaborate had been reached quite a while ago.

•

I was looking out of the car window, on my way to do an exclusive appearance at a club for new Russians. Let's not beat around the bush here and call it something it isn't – it's a bank raid, as I've heard it put. It would be a short PA at a private party and I couldn't put my heart into it. The day before I had performed a full show in a theatre to my fans, and now I was doing this to pay some bills. These appearances I try to keep low key. Ordinary fans couldn't buy tickets as it was invite only, sort of part corporate, part glitterati: and really all you are is the buffet entertainment.

The real reason you're invited is to add some status symbol presence, a touch of legitimacy. They have nothing to do with artistic integrity, which I leave at the coat check on my way in. Everyone does corporate events, or if they don't they're liars or wealthy. Take the money and schmooze.

•

So where was I?

At this private do, performing for a select audience of new Russians, meaning entrepreneurs who earn vast amounts of money from God only knows where and even God is wary of enquiring. The one thing I have found to be true is that they are obscenely decadent and extremely jaded. And like Las Vegas, they possess bad taste that only the very wealthy can have in abundance. Money is everything, most importantly it is power, and the one defining aspect of their lives is ostentatiously flaunting their wealth with every manner of status symbol imaginable. There is a Russian joke about new Russians.

A new Russian bumps into another like-minded individual in a club.

'Do you see my tie?' says one. 'It cost me 3,000 dollars.'

'You're crazy,' said the other. 'I saw it in a shop the other day for 4,000 dollars.'

BMWs, Porsches and Mercedes, always with blacked-out windows. Designer labels of the latest names from head to toe (but my Russian friend Katya said she bet their socks are full of holes).

The final accessory is of course the requisite girlfriend, traipsing three paces behind, painfully thin and with an anaemic skin. Versace dress uncompromisingly short, long legs and too much make-up covering her cosmetically enhanced looks. Cosmetic surgery has hit the big time in Moscow, and new Russian girls have embraced it with zeal – everywhere these women stagger around with airbag breasts disproportionate to their figure, resculptured noses and cheeks, and most prominent of all enormous collagen lips that look painful and swollen.

•

So here I was, on stage, looking out at a crowd made up of all the aforementioned individuals, all appearing suitably bored and staid. Sitting at one table was Anna Kournakova, another table Marat Safin, so I really did know how exclusive it was.

When it was finally over, I posed for photos with the tennis stars, swapped small talk and hurriedly left, jumped in the car with my entourage and headed homeward.

The album finally completed and the artwork underway, I returned to Moscow for a concert tribute to Alla Bayanova. This was to celebrate her eighty years of performing on stage. The concert was to be held at the Concert Hall Russia, a huge, grim Soviet-style hall normally used for classical concerts.

It was a bitterly cold January night and I watched Alla be

presented with her own star on the sidewalk of fame. Frail and suffering flu, Alla struggled in the crowd but she has stamina: at 98 years old, not only did she have the presentation, crowds and celebrations to contend with, she then had to endure the tribute show and perform as well. They don't make them like that any more. The show featured a procession of famous Russian singers and performers taking it in turn to pay homage to Alla. Throughout Alla sat on stage until by the end (which threatened to never arrive) she was buried beneath a mountain of floral tributes. Russians often invade the stage with bouquets, single red roses or photographs to sign, carried away with the drama of the occasion. It seems to matter little that a singer is performing when they approach.

It was a huge honour for me to be asked to make a contribution. Accompanied by the Orchestra Russia, I sang a solo version of the song 'Just One Chance', the audience applauding frantically as I sang in Russian – not easy, I can tell you. Then I did a rousing version of 'Heart On Snow', a traditional-style Russian song and the name of the album. The audience clapped and stomped in time, and it was one of the crowning moments of these last three years.

This felt like the right place to be in that moment – in a Russian concert hall, backed by a full orchestra, singing in Russian to Russians.

A boy from Southport, so many years, people, places, experiences. I don't know how I quite got there but all I know is that it was a long, long way from 'Sex Dwarf'.

14

A Day In Vegas

'Las Vegas: it's what the whole world would be doing on
Saturday night if the Nazis had won the war.'
— Hunter S. Thompson

•

'I am going to play Vegas.' For a moment I got the room's
attention. Well, it does sound great and to many people
playing Vegas would seem like the pinnacle of a career.

I forgot to mention that I was going to play roulette in
Vegas, not actually perform. And far from being the pinnacle
of a career it is more likely to be the final resting place for
old stars of yesteryear with a liver-spotted handful of hits
and a few gin-soaked war stories. For the surgically altered
and the seriously weird the tour stops in Vegas – forever!

Billboards bear their names in cheap neon, flashing
enticingly like gaudy prostitutes in Amsterdam windows.
Most prominent of all is Wayne Newton himself, Mr Vegas.
I'm not quite sure what he is famous for other than being
famous and being in Vegas for forty years. His face stares
out from the billboard, airbrushed complexion of pale pink,
painted hairline and a smile whiter than Jesus.

All misfits succumb to Vegas. It is the showbiz black hole,
its gravitational pull irresistible.

Surely someone can give me a home here; even down the
bill from Sheena Easton.

'Look, I can do glitter, I can do cheese – I've got some hits.'

If Sheena has a regular show on and off in Vegas, probably hiding from old Esther Rantzen who keeps trying to coax her back for a 'big time one-off special', then surely I stand an anorexically slim chance.

Vegas is a great place for the seventies and eighties stars to hide out and occasionally perform, to be remembered and embraced affectionately, for Vegas is where the past and future collide in a terrible messy glitzy collision, good taste left as roadkill.

Here is where all tours find a final resting place.

On any particular night the likes of Peter Frampton, Pat Benatar, Kenny Loggins, Jethro Tull, Boston, Boz Scaggs, BB King and Jeff Beck might be playing. I see a poster for Nancy Sinatra. Like father, like daughter – the acorn never falls far from the oak. At least you can still claim to have seen Sinatra sing in Vegas.

•

Las Vegas, an electronic oasis in the middle of the spooky old Nevada desert. How many dead bodies are buried out there in the scrub? Not to mention the Alien Spacecraft allegedly locked away in Hangar 54 in the high security area Dreamland, that secret place that's the worst kept secret – if indeed it exists at all.

I was passing through Vegas just to dredge up some old memories from yesteryear, to see how it had changed. I checked into a fifties-style hotel, complete with chalets, tennis court and a swimming pool that looked straight out of a Billy Wilder film.

I liked the hotel. It was my style, dark, old-fashioned (probably one of the oldest buildings in Vegas) but quite luxurious, and a TV that threatened to work; my room had personality though it was a little dusty. It's away from the main strip but the Hard Rock is across the road, and best of all, so is the Cheetah, the strip and lap-dance club where you can get buried in hardbody beauties if that is what tosses your salad. I was with a few friends and Neal X, my guitarist; he wanted to go to the Cheetah as soon as possible to die of pleasure in silicon. I wanted to go there too as it's featured in one of my favourite movies: Paul Verhoeven's multimillion-dollar art-house epic *Showgirls*, and to understand Vegas you have to appreciate *Showgirls*.

Now I know what you're thinking but I assure you *Showgirls* is a much misunderstood film. It is a trash culture paean to America – of sex, violence, ambition, greed, consumerism, cynicism and the ultimate vacuousness of it all, and not forgetting Versace. It is a love poem to the nineties, the most expensive exploitation film ever made. It is pure genius, and is possibly the trashiest film of all time. I suspect Verhoeven was influenced by Russ Meyer's sexploitation flicks such as *Beneath the Valley of the Ultra Vixens* and *Supervixens*, as well as the blaxsploitation films of the seventies, like Jack Starrett's *Cleopatra Jones*.

To me, *Showgirls* feels like a sublime gift, a holy work of kitsch of the highest order. With its sheer over-the-topness, *Showgirls* was bound to emerge as a cult classic.

For those of you who haven't seen it I urge you to put this book down now and get out and rent it. Well, what are you waiting for?

Alright, I know it's hard to put this book down so make a note to see it.

In the meantime here is a brief appraisal of it, to whet appetites.

Showgirls tells the simple story of Nomi Malone, a gal wanting to make it on the Vegas dancer circuit. Nomi is a wayward girl with a shady past and no-nonsense attitude –

there are loads of ridiculous outfits, nasty strip-house politics, raunchy sex scenes and gratuitous catfights.

Nomi dreams of the 'glamour' possessed by Crystal Connors, who is lead dancer in 'Goddess', a ridiculous 'erotic' dance revue at the Stardust Casino.

Blindly ambitious, Nomi seizes her chance when she pushes Crystal down a flight of stairs in order to obtain her job.

Think of it as being *All About Eve* with pasties and steroids, complete with glitzy costumes, throbbing music, trashy glamour and unapologetic tack.

Eventually and inevitably Nomi's secret comes out: you guessed it – she used to be a cheap whore – and in the end she leaves the way she came in, but not before revealing her kick-ass martial arts skills on the men who raped her best friend, make that only friend, actually make that ex-only-friend.

She hitches a ride out of town with the same man who took her there – an implausible coincidence, but by this time I suspect the writer Joel Esterhaus couldn't be bothered to think of something more convincing having spent a whole morning writing the script, and lunch at Spiga seemed a better option.

'What did you win?' the driver asks her. 'Myself,' says Nomi cryptically. Of course, she's lying. She has not grown up or learned anything – except she now knows how to pronounce 'Versace' correctly.

I dwell on this film because, having visited Las Vegas, gambled and won, and then avoided trashy drunken locals on my way back to my hotel, I can testify that it is exactly like what you see in the film. My taxi driver offered to take me to a 'titty-bar', there were slimy men on every corner giving me little cards with pictures of nude women on them, advertising some club or other, the weather was sweltering by day and freezing at night, everyone seemed to be drunk or wired or in a foul mood, and greed hung everywhere. Combine this with the bad taste that only the very wealthy can have in abundance, and there you have it. That's Vegas!

I was gladdened to see this reflected in *Showgirls*, summed up by the following line of dialogue: 'Remember that you owe neither society nor any other human being any courtesy or consideration.'

Vegas is no longer the place of Sammy, Frank or Dean. That was the sin city that danced to the beat of a crooked heart – assuming that under the slime it did have a heart. Now it is a big triple cheeseburger of a place.

I think back to my visit in 1989 when I came to film a video for my duet with Gene Pitney for the song 'Something's Gotten Hold Of My Heart'. It was a freezing cold night at the first location, a neon junkyard on the edge of the Nevada desert just south of the city, the wind whipping up a dust storm as we hit the climactic high notes. They filmed me singing while I stood on the ledge in front of a vast neon display above the entrance to the Queen casino, the reinvention of the town still only a planner's dream.

I saw now how much had changed. I always felt that the video helped propel the record to be an international number one, and so in my heart Vegas and I became a part of each other. But looking around the city now, seeing the old locations we used for filming relegated to the periphery of the new Vegas, it seemed to have little for me to relate to. It's that old familiar feeling that while you stand still, taking stock of things, the world has rushed ahead, leaving you stranded in an old familiar past. I came back to find something but instead felt lost and a little resentful that everything changed and no one bothered to let me know, like Gloria Swanson in *Sunset Boulevard* when she pushes away the sound mic, failing to fully comprehend that the era of black and white silent movies is, in all but her mind, a memory.

·

I looked out of my hotel window at the site where the legendary Sands Hotel had stood, now demolished (its very demolition was another Vegas spectacle). In its place stands one more monolithic monstrosity of modern Vegas. I sat and watched dusk slither in from the desert, and the millions of lights from the Strip flicker on. Unable to tune in the TV (the oldest ploy in the book for dissuading you from staying in), the lights of the Strip enticed me out into the night.

The Strip is effectively one street, three and half miles long, of multimillion-dollar theme hotels, and stands alone as unlike anything you will ever see anywhere else in the world. It is electrifying, exuberant, vulgar and simply the most expensively constructed movie set in the world, in which everyone is either a player or an extra in an imaginary film way over budget and schedule.

You can wander from pyramid to medieval castle by way of Venetian cityscape and Parisian landmarks, past dancing fountains, sinking galleons, exploding volcanoes and Roman gardens. Though Vegas is billed as a shrine to capitalist America, the irony is that there is very little you'd actually buy.

But the Vegas I remember and still love is Freemont Street, known since the 1940s as Glitter Gulch; it was the heart of the old swinging 'Rat Pack' Vegas. Now overshadowed despite a makeover in the nineties, it still seems run down and all but forgotten – the neon Cowboy has long since stopped waving. This was my Vegas, and I was overwhelmed by the analogies for my life and career but, what the hell, it was all just too poignant.

Experiencing Vegas is as near to damn it to being on hallucinogenic drugs without taking them. It's a mindless mind trip, utterly ridiculous in scale, totally detached from reality and so monumentally monstrous that one can only experience it first-hand and for a short period. I say this because daylight reveals it as nothing more than an illusion, albeit on a grand scale. It uses the principle of distraction – the pea under the three cups con trick no less.

Las Vegas is about gambling, nothing else. Everything it purports to offer serves a single focused purpose, and that is to lure you into their casinos. After a restless sleep full of neon dreams, cackling slot machines regurgitating quarters, I woke early, and decided to go for the 'all you can eat $4.95' breakfast buffet at the Luxor Hotel.

The Luxor is one of the city's great landmarks, an over-the-top hotel copy of the Great Pyramid, which can be seen for miles around and, claims the brochure, 'even from space' – which is not such a great claim any more since satellites can photograph llamas copulating in the Andes.

The Luxor pyramid itself is entered through an enormous ten-storey-high replica Sphinx (passing through the sphinx's sphincter into the lobby) and contains a copy of Tutankhamen's tomb (and treasures), an IMAX cinema, restaurants and, there was something else, oh yes, a casino.

The theme inside is, unsurprisingly, Egyptian, though the use of moulded resin would have been a revelation to the original builders.

The amount of effort it must have taken to create something that seems so utterly tasteless is astonishing. Its 'big smallness' underwhelms on a grand scale; it has about as much to do, in my opinion, with Ancient Egypt as treacle sponges have to do with golf.

If the pharaohs could see it now they would turn in their caskets.

•

I made my way to the breakfast buffet, and despite an in-depth search, could find nothing suitable to eat. Continuing the theme of Ancient Egypt, most of the food looked like it could have been excavated from some archaeological dig that very morning.

'How do they do it for $4.95?' I overheard one woman enquire of her husband, a man sporting a 'Chevy Chase Fan Club' T-shirt.

'Beats me,' he said.

Be warned: 'All you can eat buffets' are not so much an offer as a challenge, and the phrase should have a question mark after it.

I traipsed past what looked like piles of greasy fried eggs, charcoaled rashers of bacon, stale hash browns and under-cooked pale sausages. I waited my turn in line as obese figures padded back and forth balancing plates piled high with fried stodge, dripping in maple syrup: middle America trying to fill that emptiness, waddling back to their tables, unable to contain their glee upon discovering repeat visits are not only allowed but actually encouraged.

In a desolate bleak corner I noticed the fresh fruit buffet, nestling beside the untouched cottage cheese and low-fat yoghurt display. Making my way over I was aware of families eyeing me suspiciously, confused faces trying to grasp what the hell was I thinking? A child started crying. His mother reassured him, forking a maple-drenched waffle into his gaping and frightened mouth.

I helped myself to slices of dried-up melon and yoghurt, and took a seat in the corner. People glanced over, with expressions of pity and concern. A waitress dressed as an Egyptian slave enquired if I would like coffee. I asked if they had tea. She wasn't sure and moved off to check. I saw her speaking to a woman dressed as Nefertiti (I assumed to be the manager) and they looked in my direction suspiciously.

Moments later a cup of black tea was placed in front of me. I asked if they had any milk.

'Oh, sure,' she said, pointing to individual cartons of UHT on the table. I asked if they have any fresh milk.

She shook her head apologetically, and smiling one of those permanent pageant smiles, sloped off.

I was tempted to ask if they had any ass's milk but suspected it would only have been UHT long-life too.

Leaving the Luxor I decided to explore some of the other attractions on offer, and headed towards the New York hotel, its frontage comprised of one-third-scale replicas of the most famous landmarks on the NY skyline: the Statue of Liberty, Empire State, and so on. These are best viewed from the Manhattan Express roller coaster that speeds around them. Fortunately for the hotel, the original designers left out the Twin Towers, otherwise they would have had to demolish them – though being Vegas I'm sure they would have made a spectacle of that too.

Then across the road to Paris Hotel. Ooh la la, surrounded by French facades – the Eiffel Tower, the Arc de Triomphe – you could almost be in Paris. I say almost, but actually mean not at all. Still, I was just in time to see a Piaf look-alike 'Je Ne Regrette Rien'-ing while a line of can-can girls tussled with their frills, and a Maurice Chevalier impersonator (straw boater jauntily cocked) 'eez-hoh-eez-has' his way through 'Thank Heaven for Little Girls' whilst leering at the petticoated chorus.

Every French cliché is here. All that is missing is the smell of dog shit, French cheese ripening, sizzling garlic snails and that pungent aroma of Gauloises and bad breath. Oh, and the rudeness. Americans could never do rudeness like Parisians – mind you, nobody can.

For the Italian experience visit the Venetian Hotel, complete with the replica of the Grand Canal, the Rialto Bridge and gondolas available for rides to St Mark's Square. Or the Mandalay Bay, which caters for visitors who would rather be lying on a fake tropical island with imitation jungle foliage and an imported sandy beach than actually lying on a real one. The Mirage is built around the concept of a Polynesian village (don't even ask) and the Excalibur a theme medieval castle. You get the idea.

Soon enough it begins to wear on you, especially if like me you don't (usually) gamble. I am what is known in Las Vegas as 'the surplus to requirement 4 per cent' – those visitors who are tolerated but certainly not encouraged. I felt like that person at the orgy who's sent out to get some beers and comes back to discover the orgy has started without him and it might be rude to join in. Vegas doesn't need non-gamblers at the party spoiling it, especially when they've gone to so much effort and laid on such a spread.

It seems so perfect that the only museum in Las Vegas is Liberace's, a shrine to the man himself, conceived, created and opened by him in 1979. I had to make a visit. The museum is filled with all his famous dazzling stage costumes, now dusty and moth-eaten, standing proudly on stiff plastic mannequins (so no change there then). It is a lasting tribute to excess, flamboyance and dubious taste, and includes jewel-encrusted pianos, signature candelabras, and rhinestone-covered cars. An effeminate young man polishes diamond jewellery in a case, which upon close inspection looks like paste. The diamonds have probably long since been pawned off to pay the embalming bills, the ones he amassed while still alive, judging by some of the latter-day photos of the man, just prior to his ill-fated 'water melon' diet, which he claimed accounted for his sudden weight loss.

Wandering around this mausoleum, I noticed photos of Liberace (or Lee as he was affectionately known) with his young 'personal assistant' Scott. One particular photo shows the two of them smiling into the camera, Lee dressed in a mink coat, collar turned up, hair coiffured; Scott is in a white tunic. Lee is leaning in towards Scott, his expression affectionate and proud, whereas Scott is turned ever so slightly away from Lee, his smile awkward, his eyes glazed and pupils dilated.

I recalled a documentary about Liberace in which Scott revealed he was pressurized into undergoing cosmetic surgery so he would look like Liberace. He revealed how Liberace's own cosmetic surgery was botched, leaving him disfigured. During the interview Scott complained how Lee betrayed him and cut him out of his life after discovering his drug use. He finally revealed how horrified he had been to discover later, after their separation, that Lee had suffered from Aids all along, and never informed him.

You can see in the photo, no doubt taken after both had surgery, that they share the same rictus smile and tightening around the eyes. It must have been taken just prior to the incident in which Scott was to drive Lee on stage in a diamanté-covered Rolls-Royce. The worse for wear from drugs and drink, Scott crashed the car into the wings (which personally I think is quite an entrance). But for Lee that was the last straw. Scott had humiliated him in front of a live audience, something he was perfectly capable of doing himself.

The photo reveals an intimacy and a distance.

In one way I sympathize with Liberace, having met a few Scotts of my own. They're always the same: cute, roguish, sexy, ambitious and troublesome. They always have stars in their eyes, a trick up their sleeve, a hard-luck story, a modelling contract in the offing, a business venture that just needs backing – all they need is a break, and when it doesn't transpire, it's tears and accusations, and off to find another soft touch who might believe their hard-luck story.

There's a factory that churns them out, with brand names
Scott, Kevin or Jason.

I have an old theatrical friend who tells me, 'I got money,
a white Rolls-Royce, a house in the South of France, another
on Fire Island, a walk-in wardrobe, and in honesty need
never work again. And I've got a telephone book full of
Scotts, and they've all disappointed me, but then they'd
disappoint me if they didn't.'

> I'll be seeing you
> In all the old familiar places
> All the old familiar faces

Liberace and Las Vegas. When you haven't got that much
going for you, just give them the old razzle-dazzle.

•

I will never forget the day when I heard the news. Friday,
3 October 2003. It was like September 11th all over again.
I sat down and just shook my head in disbelief. Could it be
true? Roy Horn had been mauled by one of his white tigers
during a performance of the Siegfried and Roy show at the
Mirage Hotel.

For these two deeply tanned Bavarians, the inseparable
and ambiguous pair of magicians and Vegas royalty no less,
the curtain fell one last time.

> All shows cancelled until further notice.

I was lucky enough to see them perform their unique brand
of illusion, when I felt the essence of Siegfried and Roy,
simultaneously vulgar and disingenuous, an allure that had
an unnameable, sparkly oddness. To understand them you
need to know something of their background, according to
their press release.

Siegfried grew up in a small German town with a fear of

his strict, emotionally repressed father, while secretly longing
to study magic. His dream was to buy a giant magic book at
a local book store, but he couldn't afford it. Then, one day,
he found a five-mark note on the street and was able to buy
the book. Destiny, in other words, was calling. (Are you
buying this?)

Similarly, Roy was growing up lonely in another small
German town, depending on a pet dog for friendship. When,
one day, the dog saved him from sinking in quicksand, Roy,
too, felt a calling.

The story goes that Siegfried and Roy met on a cruise
ship in 1957. Siegfried noticed Roy performing magic tricks
for passengers and got chatting, as you do, and took Roy
back up to his cabin to show him his, hmm, pet cheetah that
he'd stowed on board, as you do, and suggested they combine their two talents. Magic and animals.

Hey presto. The rest is history, and all you need to know
is Siegfried Fischbacher and Roy WWE Ludwig Horn now
live together in the same house in Las Vegas but in separate
quarters, take separate vacations, and consider themselves
professional – not romantic – partners. Just in case you
thought otherwise.

That partnership included until recently a $60-million
Las Vegas production involving white lions and tigers, an
elephant, fifty dancers and just acres of spangly outfits and
white leather jumpsuits. This allowed them annual earnings
of $65 million, a ten-acre jungle palace and a hundred-acre
animal sanctuary in Nevada.

I remember sitting with my friend in the specially built
Vegas Theater. We could barely contain our excitement,
though it was annoying that all tables were for four persons
so we had to share ours with an elderly couple, one of whom
had dropped off already before the show had started.

Then it began, a blistering array of illusions and effects:

Siegfried and Roy battling a fifty-foot mechanical dragon; rising into the air and walking on beams of green laser light; getting dismembered and squashed and reappearing in the middle of the audience; making an elephant appear from beneath a sheet of gold satin, and then just as quickly making it disappear.

Then Siegfried flew across the auditorium whilst Roy informed us that 'we can all fly, all we need is to believe', which was not strictly true as a harness and wires seemed quite important.

They exchanged affectionate banter, Siegfried making some comments about Roy's appearance, and Roy tossing back his mullet defiantly and trying to pull an appropriate expression (any expression might have done but his extensive surgery prevented it) before flouncing off. Rumour has it that they haven't spoken off stage to each other for years. Another rumour is that Siegfried retired secretly years earlier, replaced by a younger cosmetically enhanced look-alike.

Then midway through the show the special effects ceased and Siegfried came down into the audience and performed sleight of hand card tricks, something entirely lost in this enormous auditorium. I was just about to drop off to sleep like the man seated at our table (who by now was snoring) when, Christ almighty, there was an enormous explosion on stage to indicate we were approaching their climax.

Sure enough.

Roy appeared on top of a giant silver glitterball sitting astride a white tiger. He cracked a whip and several more white tigers lumbered across the stage and reluctantly perched on ledges built into the glitterball (I don't want to suggest these big cats were drugged in any way but they looked positively lethargic – still, two shows a night, five nights a week and a weekend matinee would take it out of any tiger). Then suddenly, and I kid you not, the glitterball began to float upwards over the auditorium, complete with white tigers and Roy on it. A collective gasp issued from the audience as it began to spin above our heads. I mean, I've seen some camp moments in my life but this was mind-bogglingly up there!

As a finale we got a gushy home video showing them at home with their OTT pets.

'To make real your dreams, all you have to do is believe,' uttered Siegfried, with all the reassurance of a cult leader. 'We must love our world, nurture it and respect it.'

The more overweight the audience members, the more they oohed and aaahed, although most of them were probably imagining heading to the nearest food outlet where they would gorge on burgers grown on prairie carved from vast swathes of unspoilt South American rainforest.

I discovered that Siegfried and Roy refuse to answer any questions about their sexuality, which you wouldn't if you were straight, and claim 'we are married to our profession'. Their programme says they are absolutely not animal trainers, and must never be considered as such. Apparently Roy is a tiger from another life, which is a simple fact and cannot be disputed. And Siegfried is a magical force, and deep in the depths of his soul is the centre of the universe, because that is a fact too.

So there you have it. As normal as you or me. And just in case you doubted that they are just 'two simple men with a dream', compare your life to theirs.

They live with 55 white tigers, 38 servants, and 16 lions. Roy sleeps with the young tigers. Siegfried has a mural of himself naked, with cheetahs, on his bedroom walls. They greet people by saying, 'Sarmoti' – an acronym for 'Siegfried and Roy, Masters of the Impossible'.

The couple claim they have many friends but their friend-ship with Michael Jackson is beyond understanding. Fair enough. Mind you, they look like brothers over the skin.

Whether Roy will make a full recovery only time will tell. Siegfried says Roy is responding and communicating. 'His colour is back.'

Down the Strip at the Monte Carlo is Siegfried and Roy's nemesis, an illusionist too and in light of Roy's face-off with a tiger, poised to take their throne. His name is Lance Burton: he doesn't use white tigers. He uses white ducks, but the principle is the same – put something in a box and change it into something else. It doesn't matter whether you're changing a woman into a white tiger or a white duck. It's the same act. Sort of. Hey, don't knock it, no one's been savaged by a duck.

•

My guitarist Neal insisted that I go with him to the lap-dancing club Cheetah's, assuring me that it would be a new experience. Having seen *Showgirls* I couldn't wait to see it for real.

Now Neal knew the routine. Entering the club he said all the right things and we were shown to an exclusive table near the back but close to the stage. Drinks arrived immedi-ately and the show began.

The audience, comprised entirely of drunken vocal guys of all ages, erupted in a cheer as the first of maybe a dozen women began to pole dance, all topless, only a G-string strategically arranged covering their modesty. Maybe mod-esty isn't the right word.

The women were all incredible: all identically propor-tioned, toned, hard bodies, tiny waists and enormous silicone breasts, collagened lips and perfectly sculpted faces. All that distinguished them was their hairstyle or hair colour.

All personal characteristics that may have made them real people had gone. They were simply sex objects, not the sort of girls Germaine Greer would have over to one of her feminist literary soirées.

By this time Neal was all but overcome by it, unable to focus on one particular dancer, in awe of them all, drooling and fidgeting.

Then they left the stage and mingled with the audience, cavorting, thrusting, squatting, pouting, teasing: anything to get dollar bills shoved under the dental-floss G-string from the baying mob. Neal attracted one dancer's attention (by frantically waving a hundred-dollar bill and shouting loudly) and instantly – no, quicker than that – she was at our table, breasts thrust in his face, whispering in his ear, inviting him for a private dance. How could he refuse, he told me, his face enveloped in a wide mischievous grin.

A private dance costs $100 for five minutes in a booth. You can't touch the dancer, and you must buy her a drink. Champagne naturally.

Five minutes later Neal was back at the table eyeing up another dancer. Well, this seemed to me a great deal of money for what amounted to not very much of anything except pent-up frustration down a one-way street.

I found the whole experience fascinating. I think straight men are much the same as gay men, only the opportunity to indulge their fantasies is far more restrictive. But given the opportunity all men are just big kids: sex, sweetshops and silicone, and too much pocket money.

•

It was my last evening and my friend convinced me that I should at least have a gamble, since this is Vegas and that is what everyone does. Reluctantly I agreed, and before I knew it we were in the Hard Rock Casino and I was sitting at the roulette table. Now I need no introduction to roulette since it is my favourite casino game from years ago. It seems odd even to me that I love to gamble at roulette. Naturally I have no idea about odds and split bets but simply put chips all over the table and wait. At one point I was thousands of dollars up, but casino chips are designed to have no monetary feel to them, colourful plastic discs to play with, so you become reckless. Naturally they diminished as rapidly as they were acquired, and I called it a day and left about $500 up. I was a winner because I walked out when I was ahead. No, I was a winner because I walked out having not lost everything.

The woman sitting next to me at the table told me that Bruce Willis won $200,000 the previous night at this very table, as though I should be impressed.

'Isn't that something,' she added. 'My husband says Bruce is one hell of a lucky guy, don't you think, $200,000?'

I smiled and nodded, all the time thinking what $200,000 must mean to Bruce Willis, win or lose.

'I'd love to win that much,' she said, sliding two five-dollar chips onto the black square, hesitating, and then cautiously retrieving one. I paused to see her win $10. She was well on her way, only $199,990 to go. It seemed to escape her that in the great casino called life, Bruce had already won.

15

Los Angeles

LA Lay

•

I suppose when people think of LA they usually think of Hollywood but apparently the city has a lot more to offer than just films, though nothing springs to my immediate mind. The guidebooks say great weather, good food, a world leader in architecture, art, style and content but I'm not convinced. I'm not suggesting it's not exciting or lacking in energy, but New York appeals to me much more, given the choice.

I've never really got to know anyone that well in LA, which if I had might have helped me get acquainted with it better. But it's hard to get to meet anyone in LA who has time for out-of-town friends; keeping in touch is too much like maintenance. And then it's not who you are so much as what you can do for them. Of course, not everyone is like that, though everyone I met was, and famous, only most are not famous yet. LA is about blind optimism and ambition, everyone waiting for their moment, that one chance that will change their lives. It's not about if and who, it's about when and how, 'cos in LA everyone has enough talent to succeed, all they need is a break, and no one is going to let that pass them by.

My first and biggest problem when I spend any time in

LA is that I don't drive. Everyone drives except me. Taxis are an option but life is too short as they take forever to come, and cost a fortune simply because everything is so far away. So being unable to drive restricts you to your hotel or the immediate area. And when you do get a taxi where do you go? There is no centre as such – as Burt Bacharach so succinctly put it, 'LA is a great big freeway.'

It's all the harder these days because no one really knows who I am. Back in the eighties when 'Tainted Love' was the biggest record ever and I was a known face, everyone wanted to stop by, swap numbers and pencil in lunch. But I never felt comfortable with fame, and LA doesn't need someone like me not buying into the package. I was in town, I was well into my fifteen minutes, why wasn't I living it up, flaunting it, partying, loving myself loving people loving me in this fabulous town where shame has no name? The vice president of my record company at the time took me aside and said, 'What is it with you – are you only ever gonna order salad?'

I felt bad for everyone around me because I was a bad, bad celebrity. They wanted some glitter and all I wanted to do was tell everyone to leave me alone. I didn't give a fuck about this party or that restaurant, meeting such and such, or schmoozing up to that journalist or posing for this magazine. That was then.

Now, relegated to the One Hit Wonder slot on VH-1 and a *Behind the Music* documentary (which is another way of packaging the *Where Are They Now* format) I might just reconsider any offers. The problem is that by the time I learned not to give a fuck, neither did anyone else.

Fame, I've come to understand, is about the three following things: poverty, vanity and revenge.

I confess they are the elements that drove me. But be warned, they come back to get you in the end. Poverty drove me and now it's coming back; that's why I occasionally do weddings, bar mitzvahs and funerals – for the money. Oh, get down from there. You understand.

Vanity too was a force but paradoxically it comes with an equal measure of insecurity and in the end the only place vanity drives you is to the cosmetic surgeon.

And revenge, I tell you it fuels you because of all those people who write you off, those who stuck the boot in, before and when you were famous: and now, now they can relish your fall from grace, or disgrace in my case. Inevitably you dismissed them or insulted them on your way up and now discover they're the people who work for VH-1 or MTV and decide who gets shown. Needless to say they get their revenge. If I'd only kissed all those arses. I recall the old saying, 'If you sit on the riverbank long enough you will see the bodies of your enemies float by'. I always assumed I was the one waiting on the riverbank; see how wrong you can be.

I hated, and still hate, doing promo tours in LA more than anywhere else. Having to try to generate some enthusiasm about my latest release is an arduous and thankless struggle. I sweat and squirm in interviews as some pinched airhead with attitude and a Kmart facelift from some trendsetting magazine called *Dish* or *Slush* or some other pleased-with-itself title. So there I'd be, microphone shoved in my face, being asked questions like, 'Were you and Jimmy Somerville, you know, an item?' or 'What is Boy George really like, I mean really?'

It's all so meaningless that I find I struggle with it and end up coming over as too serious. 'And oh, that Marc Almond, oh, dull, you don't know the half, quadruple humour bypass!!'

LA publications simply want catty or bitchy soundbites, or to 'dish' the latest gossip about who's been seeing who and 'Is it true that such and such was caught in the you know where giving a certain person a you know what? I mean off the record.'

Yeah, right!

•

My hotel of choice is Le Parc (733 NW Knoll Drive), comfortable, great location, not so expensive and it has a pool on the roof. The rooms are more like studio apartments, which suits me fine. In the past I've stayed in all the famous hotels from the Mondrian, Beverly Hills, the Chateau Marmont, and the lesser-known Roosevelt (great lounge where I saw Yma Sumac perform a 'surf and turf' dinner act show).

I've come to the conclusion that Le Parc is the best for me. The famous hotels are arch, expensive and joyless; everyone parades around to be seen or catch a glimpse of a famous person, only to pretend they haven't seen them.

The other advantage Le Parc has is its location just down from Melrose, walking distance from some of the more interesting bars and a stone's throw (LA wise) from Cantner's (419 N. Fairfax Avenue). This venerable old kosher deli is open twenty-four hours a day, and that may be one of the keys to its popularity; their ageing 'waitresses from hell' certainly aren't, nor is the drab decor; even their food gets mixed reviews. But people just keep coming in droves for their huge sandwiches, low prices and rude service. I love the hot turkey sandwich smothered in gravy and cranberries, the chicken soup and the fruit sweet potato tart – what can I tell you?

LA has some great delis. Take your pick: Abbot Kinney, Millie's, Swingers, to name some great ones.

•

Now just because I'm not enamoured by LA doesn't mean
I don't like the occasional visit, especially when touring.
LA audiences are incredibly enthusiastic and loyal, and it
can still be thrilling. For me it must be work – hotel paid
for, making money, an excuse to be there, no cost incurred
and three days max.

I have also come to make, over the decades, and despite
my earlier complaints, a few friends, and I count Chi Chi
LaRue among them: a unique generous person who almost
defies description. A larger than life drag queen, now a
hugely successful porn film director, which is a remarkable
achievement for anyone, let alone 'a fat ugly drag queen'.

While in LA, Chi Chi invited me to be a fluffer on his
latest movie currently in production but I declined, appalled
that he would even suggest such a thing. A fluffer in case
you are unfamiliar with the term is a behind-the-scene man
or woman (depending on the movie) who assists the porn
actors to get erections. How this is achieved is, well, by any
means necessary. I'll tell you, I'm sure many of you can
think of quite a few worse jobs than that, given the time.
Mind you, since Viagra came along, it's all but killed off the
fluffing industry overnight.

So no sooner had I put the phone down to Chi Chi than
I got a call from another porn director I know. Ten minutes
later this said person arrived in his jeep at my hotel, accompanied by his latest protégé (a fresh-faced straight-off-the-
Greyhound bus young man), and all of us drove off towards
downtown LA. The director, a middle-aged dumpy fella,
shall remain nameless. So while we were motoring along he
talked incessantly, one hand on the steering wheel and the
other holding a cigarette while gesticulating wildly. Yacking
ten to a dozen, he drove so erratically I suspected he was
high as a kite on cocaine (the white crusts in the corner of
his dry mouth all but confirming my suspicion). He

explained that his new protégé (the young man in the back) was going to star in a series of porn films he was planning. The protégé, who had a name, Rich, smiled enthusiastically.

'He's going to be a star.'

I'm thinking what an old corker of a cliché is this guy spinning the kid.

'I've got this great idea for this movie. Rich is gonna play a bellboy, and he gets stuck in the hotel lift with two nasty black guys, and suddenly, the lift stops between floors, and it must be a power cut 'cos the air conditioning's gone off and it's getting hotter and hotter, and so they take their clothes off and then Rich gets . . .'

Let's leave it there. You'll have rent it to see what happens next, if and when it ever gets made or released.

The last time I met the director was in Chicago a month back. I'd met some of his 'stars' in the making then too. They came to meet me in the dressing room after my show and signed a copy of their latest video offering *Jumping Bail 2* (a sequel to their first hot-ass flick, so I assumed they were recaptured). I'd decided not to take the video back to England with me, the cover being just a little too explicit. That was then.

But now, back in the jeep we were speeding down the freeway to God knows where. I tentatively asked the director what became of the porn stars I'd met back in Chicago, but immediately regretted asking. He tensed up.

Silence.

'Gone. I only know the blond one went back his dad's farm in Virginia. Decided he didn't want to be famous, the stupid shit. He's the reason I came to California. Fucking threatened to press charges, made some nasty allegations, you believe that?'

I thought it best to keep quiet after that.

The jeep pulled off the freeway and into a car park.

Turning, he informed me that his new project was a musical venture. A boy band.

Oh my God, I'm thinking.

He then told me that he wanted my opinion on them, and had arranged a short performance for me to cast a critical eye over their talent.

I tried to explain that I wasn't the right person to criticize anyone but he was insistent and so I reluctantly agreed.

Next thing I know we're out of the jeep and I'm in a studio sitting in front of the band, a pleasant enough group of young men; quite ordinary, actually, not the sort you would imagine young girls breaking their hearts over. Then they performed several songs for me, and throughout I tried to keep a sincere expression, occasionally nodding, drumming my fingers and tapping my feet to the beat. The director kept looking at me and I kept nodding approval and expressions of amazement.

They finished and I applauded politely and then, then I lied through my teeth.

'Great, really great. You guys are . . . really . . . wow!' all the while trying to find something positive in what I'd just seen, which to be fair was neither good nor bad, just nothing special and in fact I'd already forgotten it.

But all eyes were trained on me, waiting for more critique.

'Great, really great. Whatever that special something is, I think maybe, just maybe you guys have it. Just don't give up, keep writing songs, keep playing wherever you can, get as much experience and keep fine tuning.'

They hung on my every word.

Then the lead singer asked, 'What could we improve on?'

That caught me out.

'Improve on? Uhm . . .'

They all leaned forward, intently waiting for whatever pearls of wisdom I was about to dispense.

'You could . . .' I hesitated. I wanted to say the world needs great mechanics and great waiters, there's no shame in it. 'You could maybe learn a few moves, a couple of dance steps. You thought of that?'

That is really weak, Marc, I'm thinking, but hell it worked. They were suddenly excited by this incredible idea that plainly, and to my utter astonishment, had never occurred to any of them.

The director added, 'Yeah, Christ, that is great, Marc, just like New Kids on the Block, eh?'

But the group looked perplexed at who New Kids on the Block might be.

•

The sights. Forget Beverly Hills – sure, it's glitzy, sleek, manicured, but it's got no chutzpah. And then consider how many extravagant shops can you not afford to shop at and how many opulent homes can you know you'll never have. Don't torture yourself. A friend in all seriousness said I should go and explore Santa Monica and Venice. People bike, surf, skate, work out, there are mountains that roll down to the seashore, it's a beautiful place to wander. My friend said it has some great historical architecture dating back from the 1970s. Can you believe that? Wow, that old?

Every time someone tells me about what to see or do, it almost always involves shopping.

Or their shock that I haven't visited Universal or Disneyland! Expressions of utter disbelief – 'You gotta do Disney – everyone does. It's so much fun.'

I just don't buy into that.

Or, people suggest, why not try the SwapMeet where 'one person's trash is another's treasure', or at least I think it was that. 'It is so much fun, you could swap your old lava

lamp for, say, a KerPlunk game.' Hey, how much fun is
that?

•

Rich, the protégé (not forgotten already, the up and coming
porn star), took me on a bar crawl of dubious haunts near
my hotel. He had broken free from his Svengali for the
evening and offered to drive me around.

First thing you notice about bars in LA is they are half
empty. Since it is illegal to smoke inside, everyone's crowded
on the pavement outside smoking.

Rich first took me to a hustler bar called Numbers,
notorious for its upmarket hustlers and sagacious punters.
The bar was decorated in black glass, mirrors and chrome,
and felt positively eighties. Situated on the first floor and
entered by a lift, it had a small, seated veranda, long bar and
dimly lit restaurant. The clientele fell into two categories,
separated by at least two generations. The hustlers, casually
dressed in designer labels, sat around sipping beers and
courting the elderly gentlemen as they tried to catch their
eye. Several had already made acquaintance and sat chatting
or overordering in the restaurant.

The owner, flouncily dressed with tinted hair, held court
from his stool at the end of the bar, snapping orders at
waiters and greeting regulars. There was an air of private
club about the place. I bought a drink and sat.

Rich moved to the bathroom and while gone several
young men tentatively approached, politely introducing
themselves – Scott from Texas, Scott from Anaheim and Abe
from out West. I politely made my excuses and they politely
moved off. An elderly man, dressed in Ralph Lauren, waved
to the owner as he left escorted by two young men, a private
agreement having been negotiated quietly over dinner.

To the casual observer it would be difficult to recognize the discreet manoeuvres and rituals enacted out here nightly. Rich, having returned, pointed out to me who was available and how much someone might expect to pay for their various services, should they be so inclined. For the record, between $100 and $200 would secure companionship for between an hour and the whole night. This would naturally be cash in advance and non-refundable, so whatever it is you have in mind needs to be clarified in advance, to avoid any misunderstanding. Rich informed me that most of the men were known to the owner and therefore 'quite' trustworthy, meaning I suppose they might rob you, but wouldn't cut you into small pieces and dump them in Griffith Park.

From there we went to another bar, Hunter's, on Santa Monica Boulevard, which I'm told is the other end of the market. Now Hunter's is a hustler bar too, but in quite a different league. It looks like a typical LA bar, pool table, pinball machine, sawdust on the floor. But the hustlers were, how can I put this, nasty-looking motherfuckers. The gay description would be 'rough trade' but that doesn't come close. They swaggered menacingly, eyes glazed, stoned expressions, swigging beers. Several had taken their tops off, their torsos scarred and tattooed.

Some sat with elderly men, begging drinks or boasting about some deal or other. There was a sense of desperation and danger in the air; at any moment a fight could flare up or a punch be thrown.

Rich assured me that most of the hustlers were on crack and just looking for enough money to buy their next fix. Most would let you give them a blow job for $10 out back in the car park, or you could take them back for $20, but I'm thinking take them back where? Class acts. He told me that most of them were not as bad as they looked, which I found hard to believe.

Suddenly two Puerto Rican girls came into the bar, each carrying infants. The girls started to shout in Spanish at a couple of the guys playing pool – and though I couldn't understand what they were saying, the body language suggested it was about getting your asses home, stop stealing the child support money to buy crack and start putting food on the table.

The guys grabbed the girls, dragging them outside where they continued to argue, the girls eventually tussling with them, the babies screaming by now. Moments later the two hustlers were back playing pool, their girlfriends having stormed off. Rich explained that most of the hustlers are 'gay for pay'.

As we left one of the two playing pool grabbed my arm tightly.

'You wanna blow me for twenty dollars?' he asked with a Texan drawl, then added, 'Or both of us for thirty dollars? How about it?'

His friend looked up from cueing his ball at the pool table, and winked.

I was taken aback at the frankness of the offer.

He continued, unabashed, 'We got twenty inches between us.'

Still considering his shot, his friend smiled, front teeth missing, and nodded, confirming his friend's claim.

I politely declined. He smiled a 'well, it's your loss' kinda smile, let go of my arm and returned to his pool game.

Outside in the warm air I felt a sense of relief.

Now even my maths is not great but as we climbed back in the car I kept thinking about twenty inches divided by two, and whichever way you figure it, at least one of them was going to have an impressive tool.

•

The next day was show day (that's why I'm in LA) and as always before a show I felt anxious and apprehensive. It's a black cloud that worsens as show time nears: nerves overcome me and feelings of doubt engulf me right up until I walk out on stage, and then they subside and it all makes a kind of sense as to why I put myself through it. I should have known that LA would be a great show, well attended and enthusiastic, but it's hard to convince myself beforehand, regardless of where I'm playing. An additional pressure is playing shows like LA where you know familiar faces are out in the audience. I want to do well, and I want them to have a good time, and I want them to see me doing a good show and see the audience loving it. I want their appreciation and the audience's reaction because, oh don't get me started – those waves of unconditional love that tell me 'I'm Still Here'. And my sense of relief at being told it was sold out. After all, isn't hell a half-full auditorium?

The day after a show has its difficulties too as you scrutinize and relive the performance in your mind, over and over. And when the tour manager comes in and informs me the show was reviewed in various papers, my heart sinks and I have to remind him that I don't want to know about any reviews. Then he sits in the corner and the conversation follows the same routine:

ME: Why did you tell me it was reviewed?
TOUR MANAGER: I thought you might want to see them.
ME: No.
TOUR MANAGER: But they're great.
ME: No!
TOUR MANAGER: OK, sorry I mentioned it.
But by then he can't unmention it.
ME: I'm not interested.
TOUR MANAGER: Sorry.
Silence. Curiosity gets the better of me.

ME: How great?

TOUR MANAGER: On the whole, great.

ME: What do you mean on the whole? Some are not great
then?

TOUR MANAGER: You want to read them or not?

ME: Which one didn't like the show?

TOUR MANAGER: A couple thought it . . .

ME: A couple now . . .? So more than one didn't like the
show?

And so it goes on. All I'm able to do is focus on the
negative, regardless of how much positive press there may
be. I take anything negative as a personal affront to me,
whereas anything positive is simply accurate. And inevitably
if the review is glowing in every aspect, then you can be sure
as hell I'll hate the accompanying photo – an unflattering
close-up side shot of me midway through a note, face
contorted, sweaty and looking terrible.

There's no pleasing some people, or more to the point,
no pleasing me.

•

They don't call it 'the City of Angels' for nothing.

Life is lived large in Los Angeles.

To relax, Neal drove us around Hollywood on the death
tour, a look at all the places where those famous names met
their final filmmaker. A memorable death as a star is essential to extend posthumous popularity – in fact death in LA
is entertainment, and though death in Hollywood is much
the same as death practically anywhere else, here it is just
more so. If you think about it, many dead celebrities do
seem much more dead than regular dead people – and the
place and cause of death endlessly fascinates, especially if
accidental, suicidal or in particular homicidal.

'That's where River Phoenix died,' said Neal, pointing

out the Viper Room Club. And further on, the site of Roman Polanski and wife Sharon Tate's home, scene of one of Manson 'family's' most brutal murder rampages. The house was demolished in 1994, but we can imagine.

Up the tree-lined street where Jamie Lee Curtis babysat in *Halloween*, and still further to Jayne Mansfield's pink palace where no one actually died but which is now owned by Englebert Humperdink. I don't know if that means anything but it seems to.

Then past the suburban residential hotel where Divine died in his sleep.

I asked if we could go to the house where Nicole Brown Simpson and Ron Goldman were murdered over in Brentwood, but I was told by Neal it's too far to drive, and apparently the neighbourhood association is quite active when it comes to deterring sightseeing. He told me the house too had been demolished.

We drove past lavish houses set back in austere grounds behind enormous gates, each bearing the sign 'SECURITY – ARMED RESPONSE', and CCTV cameras on every pillar and post recording every move, guarding against the next psycho who feels a murderous need to disembowel Janet Leigh or decapitate Cher.

We pulled over for lunch at Ubon, a très chic restaurant, a multimillion-dollar shrine to extremely conspicuous consumption located in the heart of Beverly Hills. I warmly recalled seeing it overrun with molten lava in Tommy Lee Jones' film *Volcano*. Needless to say we couldn't get a table since we hadn't made a reservation in the mid-nineties.

Then it was on to the Hollywood Forever Memorial Park, which certainly lives up to its name. I think cemeteries and death are great tonics when facing a midlife crisis, for getting you out of your malaise, and nowhere has better ones than LA.

Looking north through its front gates, you can see the Hollywood sign up atop the Hollywood Hills and, looking south, the historic back lot of the Paramount Studios. Interred throughout the cemetery grounds are some of the most famous stars in the history of Old Hollywood, including Rudolph Valentino, Douglas Fairbanks, Nelson Eddy and Tyrone Power.

This is also an old cemetery, filled with tall, old-fashioned headstones and towering monuments, including a few unusual ones shaped like obelisks and rocket ships.

My other favourite cemetery is the Pierce Bros Westwood Village Memorial Park. At this tiny site you will find the final resting places of some of the most famous stars in Hollywood, including Dean Martin, Natalie Wood, Jack Lemmon, Mel Torme, Peggy Lee, George C. Scott, Burt Lancaster and Truman Capote.

So many great names, so many memories buried. If you had to choose only one Hollywood cemetery to visit this is the one. Popular with the show biz crowd (especially since Marilyn was buried here). All the crypts are quite plain, but there is one, slightly darker than the rest – stained by the multitude of fans who have touched and kissed it. The small marker reads: 'Marilyn Monroe: 1926–1962'.

A final resting place among the stars here reportedly costs about $22,000. There is still one remaining crypt on Marilyn's wall but it is reportedly priced at over $80,000.

But it costs nothing to visit.

•

Finally we drove up towards the Beverly Hills Hotel to visit the one place I needed to pay my respects to: the infamous toilet where George Michael was arrested by that more attractive than average LA police officer. Even as public toilets go, it is one of the strangest. It is situated on a roundabout, the grass well manicured, the flower beds well tended, just by a sign emblazoned with a 'City of Beverly Hills – The Will Rogers Memorial Park'. At first one might be mistaken in thinking this could be the place, exposed, in this rich area, this showpiece park. But no, there it is, a shrine to a decimated career. A small white-painted public convenience, not at all conducive to what you might imagine. I ventured inside. It is well maintained, almost pristine. Not at all like its British counterparts where gay men loiter at urinals, forever shaking and pretending to pack up, or waiting outside at the bus stop for that bus that never comes.

How surreal that image must have been of one of the world's most famous stars putting on a burlesque show for one of LA's finest. I stood in there taking in the air of history. It seemed such an unlikely setting for such a calamitous crash. But that is the nature of fame and the fragility of it. The transformation of George Michael's fame. He walked in one bright sunny afternoon a superstar with his reputation and credibility intact, and was dragged out in handcuffs quite a different man (quite literally dragged out of the closet).

'Little strokes fell great oaks.' American proverb.

The singer told police he had been searching for his lottery ticket, which must be up there as the lamest excuse ever. His life from that moment on would always be punctuated by 'that incident', and it would overshadow so much of what he had achieved.

He may claim now it was the best thing that happened to his life, as it forced him to be honest, and maybe he believes that, or maybe he really was looking for his lottery ticket. It was, after all, a multiple rollover draw.

LA is a cruel town. I've experienced it first hand. Yesterday counts for nothing. It is where you are today that matters, and you're either on your way up, at the top, or you're just nowhere, a nobody that counts for nothing.

Everyone who settles in this city does so because they want to live the dream, otherwise you wouldn't be here. It is that simple.

The pressure to succeed and stay at the top is what drives everyone. It is this naked ambition that makes people disregard much of what we consider important values in life. Traits such as ruthlessness and callousness are acceptable, a necessary part of the process that is succeeding – it really doesn't matter who you screw, who you fuck over, whether you manipulate, lie or cheat: so long as you get to the top no one cares how you got there, what you did to get there (so long as you're not found out) or what you do to stay there.

Like I said, the question on everyone's lips is, 'What can you do for me?'

And that is why so much goes horribly wrong for so many, why there is so much craziness. It is this dark side of the city's psyche that obscures the light, and that is why I'm fascinated but ill at ease with it.

It is a car accident of a town. It is sex and drugs and money and scandal – it is excess.

And I look back at the height of my fame (that brief eclipse) and think how lucky I was that I was not seduced by LA. How easy it might have been for me to live here, as so many British musicians do, get forever caught up in recording an album between lazing, hungover, by the pool; imperceptibly (only to me though) balloon in weight, grow a ponytail, a whole new look in fact, get a drug habit I couldn't afford and stagnate. Maybe I would have stayed in the closet and dated a shampoo model – you know, one of those mutually beneficial arrangements.

But eventually the album would be finished, having settled on an LA middle of the road adult-orientated rock sound, slick production, tracks about Freeways and Love Hustling, all very eighties and FM. A celebration of crass excess.

> I have a mansion
> Forget the price
> Ain't never been there
> They tell me it's nice
>
> – 'Life's Been Good', Joe Walsh

Los Angeles is creative suicide and commercial death. Even if the album sells well you've spent so much in the process of recording it, on everything from drugs, sushi, hustlers or hookers, more drugs, rehab, suites at the Sunset Marquis, weekends in Vegas, different drugs, limos, tattoos, hair extensions and Harleys that you can't ride, that you can never recoup costs.

Then you're out drinking and snorting, thinking it doesn't get much better than this, and the next thing you know you wake up in the Mount Sinai ER having overdosed. The paramedics revive you but you've suffered brain-damage. As for your career that couldn't be resuscitated, pronounced dead on arrival. The best that can happen to you is if they do the humane thing and turn off the life support machine for good.

You know, standing in Los Angeles airport checking in, I thought of what Groucho Marx said: 'I've had a wonderful time, but this wasn't it.'

16

Mexico City

Mariachi Maelstrom

•

Sometimes my management gets an offer for me to do something in which the money is terrible but it may still interest me. I'll give you an example: an offer to appear in Mexico City, all expenses paid including club class flights, five-star hotel, et cetera, but not much else. They suggested I could make it a holiday by staying a week extra. Having never been to Mexico and since the offer was the only one I've had from there, ever, I agreed to do it. Besides, the midlife crisis was plaguing me so the chance to visit somewhere new might help shake it, or at least take my mind off it. A new place, new inspirations and where better, I tell myself, than Mexico City.

I recalled my childhood sitting in the dingy school library reading up on the Aztecs, imagining myself standing on the Pyramid of the Sun. Now at last I could fulfil a lifelong ambition, to be reborn in the blood of a red Mexican sunset . . . Well, you get the idea. Besides, hiding in the library meant a bully-free zone. I think it was something about the sacrifices that stuck in my mind, the appeal of imagining bodies cut open on the altar of the pyramid, hearts torn out and the blood running down the temple steps. Now that would be something . . .

•

Arriving at Mexico City airport, looking out of the plane window at the mountains and arid terrain, the view was quite extraordinary and beautiful. Customs collected pointless forms and searched luggage, as I struggled to imagine just what anyone would smuggle into Mexico.

We met up with our promoter. He seemed to be on some weed or other because he was dancing to a different beat at quite another party from us. He had that Latin laid-back attitude to life – everything was mañana, schedules were improvised, nobody showing any concern for lateness or lack of organization, or even giving the impression of knowing what they were doing.

I adore drives from airports into cities. The sprawling adobe houses gradually gave way to narrow streets, widening avenues and boulevards of glass and concrete, lush green parks and palms – from extremes of poverty and wealth, from shacks into lush sprawling colonial houses, ultra modern apartments, derelict lean-tos, all mixed together, haphazardly, in a crazy conglomeration.

I noticed the pollution stinging my eyes and throat, and this was only March, so it was difficult to imagine what it must be like in the height of summer. We were instructed by our driver to keep the windows closed and doors locked.

Upon arriving at the Grand Hotel Melia, a modern five-star characterless monstrosity, the madness continued unabated. No rooms had been reserved and the promoter had disappeared. I found a seat in the vast modern lobby and tried to relax and contain my frustration. Two hours later I was taken to my room on the twentieth floor, a corner suite with glass walls and an astonishing view across the city, the mountains in the distance.

Mexico City covers a vast flat plateau, apparent from the view. There are few tall buildings, being on a fault line I imagine, our hotel being one of the highest. Our driver told us about the devastating earthquake of 1985 and how our hotel was built to withstand a similar such quake, so not to worry; 'well, that's what they claim,' he adds laughing, 'but who knows if it will really.'

I kept being told that Mexico City is a dangerous place, and that I'd be ill-advised to go out on a night. But when did I ever listen to advice? Besides, the place was crawling with police. I mean literally dozens on each street corner, with different coloured uniforms with different amounts of braid and many of them heavily armed, quite a few who had meaningful jobs such as standing at an entrance of a construction site and making sure nobody without authorization entered.

I felt, if not safe exactly, certainly not at threat from being mugged or robbed.

There were zillions of undigested impressions in my mind as I looked around. Sometimes it seemed that every other building was ancient and had its own history. It reminded me a bit of Vienna or Rome. European culture is noticeable in the architecture of many buildings, street names and monuments. At other times of Barcelona, or Rio. Driving around on a balmy night through street upon street of open-fronted stores selling colourful plastic toys, household goods or motor parts, it reminded me of Bangkok, especially seeing the endless cantinas serving hot food to people sitting on the paving.

•

I turned on the TV in my room and CNN were reporting on the continuing War on Terrorism, which naturally would have no end in sight, much to the delight it seemed of the news channels. It was presented with all the subtlety of a mini series, complete with alarming images and computer-generated graphics, a sensationalist spectacle, including a piece entitled 'In Saddam's Torture Chamber'. This was intercut with those annoying on-the-spot reports brought via video-cellphone, all blurred green night-vision images, blinding flashes and reporters cowering. Every fifteen minutes the same loop of news, over and over – I was hooked and could barely bring myself to leave the hotel room. Why is it that whenever I go away, somewhere a war is raging – all you can think of is, oh God, the locals are gonna hate us. Since Britain is allied to the US and George Bush is warmongering all over the globe, it bodes badly.

> Along comes George Bush Senior and it's war
> Then it's Clinton and hell it's good times and shopping
> And then it's George (Dubya) Bush and it's war again
> Christ these Bush wars are gonna kill us.
>
> – Kiki and Herb

•

The first day in any new city when you venture out of the sanctuary of your luxury hotel (or your hostel), and tentatively take your first steps is great. And since you aren't immediately mugged within a block, you gain confidence and, what do you know, within a couple of hours you're exploring back streets and markets like you've always lived there, recklessly ignoring any advice and throwing caution to the wind. Venturing around on foot, I soon discovered, is great in Mexico City. Sure it feels dangerous, and threatens to engulf you in the chaos at any moment, but it feels alive.

Mexicans are overwhelmingly Catholic, and religious symbolism is ever-pervasive, the uniquely Mexican image of the Virgin of Guadeloupe everywhere. Catholic iconography is to be found from street corners and restaurants to taxi cabs and hotels. Churches are everywhere, all alight with candles and incense and low mumbling of prayers from old ladies clutching their rosaries. Outside the entrance stalls sell all sorts of religious artefacts, from plastic figurines of the saints through to flashing 3D portraits of Christ. Catholicism and kitsch, bedfellows. Being a sucker for this kind of tack I bought it by the bagful.

My favourite place to take breakfast is the dining room in the House of Tiles, one of the most beautiful buildings in the city. It's set inside a glorious tiled house with murals adorning the interior, but most importantly for me you can get tea and toast. I suspected that Mexican food and I were not going to be compatible. As I can't eat onions, peppers, chillies, garlic or anything too hot, what am I doing here?

One of the most interesting historical sites in Mexico City is the Zócalo (the main square), which is surrounded by some extraordinary architecture, including one of the most impressive structures, the Mexico City cathedral. It towers over Zócalo Square. The cathedral interior is incredible – nearly every surface is covered with carved plaster painted with gold leaf. Images of the saints or the suffering Christ are located throughout the church surrounded by the offerings of lighted candles, flowers and the compelling baroque art. And if that is not dramatic enough, the cathedral is actually sinking into the soft clay, the structure already lopsided.

It was just after lunch and back outside Zócola Square was not very busy, a few coaches off-loading groups of tourists. Traders sat around the edge of the cathedral, offering up their services (electricians, plumbers, joiners). But at night it took on quite a different feel, strange and crazy: colourful locals tout, singers, traders, hustlers, petty thieves, very, very dodgy types, from harebrained eccentrics to the downright dangerous. An assault on the senses, or a bodily assault if you're not careful, by the desperadoes who mill around. Of course it's the edginess that makes it vibrant. No wonder the cathedral is trying to bury itself. I imagined the ghost of Montezuma dragging it downwards, if he has time between inducing earthquakes or contaminating the water.

Poverty is everywhere. Beggars and invalids, mothers with babies and outstretched hands. Junkies hanging around the fountain, defecating on the ground and washing themselves in filthy water; or the all too common sight of kids inhaling solvent from plastic tubes tucked around their fists, their gait slouching and skin dulled, with glazed eyes and tired expressions. Not isolated incidents but commonplace, far too widespread for the police to control or find motivation to care.

•

I should, I suppose, tell you a bit about the show (that annoying thing spoiling my holiday), since that was why I was there at all. I arrived at the venue, a vast concrete edifice of a place, which threatened to hold around two thousand people. There was no sound set up, no monitors, no lights to speak of, and DJ decks dominated the stage. Eventually several reluctant crew managed to set up a sound system, but in such a way that caused the microphone to feedback. At my insistence they reluctantly set up a few lights, but nobody seemed in any way concerned, and the language barrier created the final insurmountable hurdle. The futility of it soon dawned on me, and I just surrendered and hoped for the best.

As it transpired the show was far worse than I'd even dared imagine, the sound system squealing, and the volume up near number 11 on a beatbox. The few lights I had insisted on broke and so I performed my set in semi darkness. Still, I've learned to be an old hoofer, a pro in such circumstances, and pioneered onwards towards the encore.

I focused on the positive, which was that at least no one

had turned up. It might have been easier just to take the few who had back to my hotel for dinner. All right, I exaggerate: there were maybe a couple of hundred people in this vast cavern. To give them credit, they were enthusiastic, jumping up and down and singing along. Like I said, I'm a professional – I'll play to ten thousand one night and a hundred the next, even if the latter numbers are more common than the former these days, and they'll both get the same show.

Apparently the low attendance was due to the lack of promotion, because Timo Mass, the legendary German DJ superstar, was on the bill with me and between us we should have had a few more people than this paltry (though adoring, and I love them for it) few. Anyway, seeing the size of the audience, or lack of it, Timo was having a Germanic hissy fit backstage, enraged and goose-stepping around because no one had turned up and looking (as I always do) for someone to blame.

The promoter had conveniently disappeared, and my manager was chasing him to get payment or threatening to pull the next night's show. Yes, there was to be a second night of this fiasco. As it turned out the second night was much better: word had got around and there was a decent crowd.

•

It was the morning after the night before, and I was trying to sleep in my hotel room but I could hear a rowdy demonstration down on the street below. Gays against the war. I checked on CNN quickly to ensure the war was still going on, and yep, they were right. There was the usual gay whistle-blowing, lesbian placard-waving, and up front a straw effigy of what I assumed to be George Bush (but looked more like George Melly). Up the street is the US Embassy (their intended destination), they were about to clash with another antiwar demo, only this one was not gay and somewhat more volatile. Suddenly the two demos were shouting abuse at each other and only a cordon of police prevented a clash (they are, after all, agreed on the antiwar stance, though nothing else). Violence was threatening to erupt and the irony was lost on all of them.

Since I had arrived there had been demonstrations every day. It seemed the war had really upset people. Mexico was furious with the US, who in turn were angry by the lack of support from their neighbour and threatening punishment by cutting aid and visas, and just about everyone was pissed off with everyone else. Hey, what can you do? What I always do. Take a walk.

A walk in Chapultapec Park.

From the air, it was easy to see the greenery of Chapul- tapec Park as the plane turned over the city. I recalled it stood in sharp contrast to the grey urban expanse surround- ing it.

One of the biggest city parks in the world, Chapultapec is more than a playground. Besides accommodating picnick- ers on worn-away grass under centuries-old trees, it has canoes on the lake; jogging and bridle paths; vendors selling balloons, souvenirs and a rickety miniature train. Food stalls sell meat on sticks, fresh juices and enormous bags of nachos smothered in a glutinous chilli sauce – it's an assault on the senses, a carefree place full of happy families and a world away from Shock and Awe befalling our times. But watch out for the pickpockets who slip in and out of the crowds, angelic faces whose eyes dart about, searching out the oppor- tune pocket or handbag to rifle through.

The park dates from the 1420s, when Aztec kings created the first nature reserve in the Americas. Sort of AztecLand. It is home to Chapultapec Zoo (greatly improved since the day Keiko the whale, star of *Free Willy*, found fame and was released reluctantly, only to return voluntarily to captivity, where he died). The zoo was a pleasant surprise, green and lush, and the animals seemed in excellent condition and well cared for, especially when I think of other zoos I've visited, like Bangkok and St Petersburg, which were disturbing. It has three giant pandas, which loll around like brown bears that have had a quick daub of white paint.

One of my favourite places of all in Mexico City is the house of the artist Frida Kahlo, now a museum to her. It is a large blue residence, high-walled. You enter the courtyard, and discover an oasis of tranquillity. It contains a miniature pyramid, complete with steps and statues, and all sorts of cats dozing in the shade or on the steps. Pre-Hispanic statuettes and large seashells are set into the walls. Her house is now a repository of masterpieces by Latin America's greatest female painter.

The kitchen is a riot of colour, done in yellow and blue ceramic tiles. The ever-present Mexican theme of death is here, with giant papier-mâché skeletons.

Frida's husband, famed Mexican muralist Diego Rivera, collected retablos, and one wall is entirely covered with them. Art by her husband and other artists is part of Frida's own collection.

But it is the personal artefacts, the private collections of treasures, that are the most intimate and revealing, filling the walls and shelves. There is a tiny child's bedroom upstairs, the bed made up for the child they never succeeded in having, Frida having suffered numerous miscarriages. You can wander the house, sit in the shaded garden, and lose yourself in the utter simplicity. And her ghost is there with you. She was crippled as a child in a bus accident (which drove a piece of iron through her pelvis into her back) and struggled with the effects of this accident and the pain it caused for the rest of her life, undergoing thirty-five operations, most of them on her spine and her polio-deformed right foot.

Frida Kahlo had a difficult marriage to Rivera and her injuries kept her bed-ridden sometimes for months and in a state of constant pain, resulting in pain-killer addiction and the amputation of her right leg from gangrene. Despite her failing body, Kahlo endeavoured to maintain the old ways of joy, excitement and drama. What a woman, and my point is that when you sit in this garden, it seems haunted by the pain and joy of her life. For me, it felt like a spiritual peace, utterly exhilarating.

She died shortly after her one and only public exhibition; she just had to really. She was truly a great artist because you can get her work on key rings, tea towels, sets of mugs and even computer mouse mats – and that's when you know you've made it.

Another fascinating, kind of related museum worth visiting is the bunkerlike Leon Trotsky Museum, where the Trotskys lived in exile and he was assassinated in 1940 (Frida is said to have had a liaison with Trotsky). Imagine saying to people, have you met the neighbours, the Trotskys.

•

For me Mexico means magic. Not magic like Siegfried and Roy but magic like voodoo black magic, Dennis Wheatley and curses, hexes and potions. And where else to go but the Sonora witchcraft market, one of the top spots in the world to tune into your white, black or voodoo scene.

While there are good doctors and conventional hospitals in Mexico City, many of the locals would rather try witchcraft lotions and potions before they head down to the local doctors. And it seems that the witchcraft business is booming. At the Sonora witchcraft market you will find some of the more obscure and traditional remedies that claim to help everything from ulcers, bronchitis, losing weight, getting back or having revenge on a lover, or even turning them homosexual (I think that is considered revenge and not a plus).

The first thing I noticed about being there was that I seemed like the only non Mexican ballsy enough to go. Eyes follow you everywhere. It is a veritable labyrinth of passages, a fusion of unfamiliar smells and sights – stalls of brightly coloured plastic household goods, charms, saints and gods, burning candles, piles of incense sticks, wooden crosses decorated with animal skins, exotic feathers, devil masks and painted skulls.

Strange ingredients in stores include rattlesnake skins, desiccated hummingbirds (what else would you do with hummingbirds but desiccate them?) and dried fox skins, as well as the live articles like iguanas, frogs and squirrels to make up the necessary spells. If you don't fancy toiling over a boiling cauldron yourself, ready-made concoctions are available by the phial full, or bottle if stronger magic is required.

The locals eyed me up quizzically, amused, intrigued by my tattoos. This was one place I wouldn't want anyone upset by my presence, the voodoo dolls hanging in bunches, warning me what might be my fate.

But I discovered the only real magic here was making my money disappear, as I bought mumbo-jumbo junk and satanic figurines, the sort of thing I swore I wouldn't clog my life up with any more. A clay figurine of Chango the God of Thunder sits cross-legged looking at me through red twinkling eyes, and a giant painted skull laughs mockingly. All that is needed is the rhythm of beating drums and a kaleidoscopic effect circa some seventies Hammer film with me (looking like Simon Ward) dressed in the typical 1800s costume but with a 1970s variation on it (long ruffled sleeves, et cetera), and I'd be spirited away into spasms and incantations.

Sweat ran down my face as I suddenly came across a grinning money skull, fur still attached. A smiling Mexican woman made me a concoction that would help me sleep – but for how long? Even the overpowering smell of lavender and camomile was making me drowsy.

For your own health and concerns about animal cruelty and preserving endangered species it's probably best not to participate in this strange place. But it is one of the more exotic markets of the world. I prefer it even to the souks of Marrakesh (where you really do put your life in their hands) and the Indian market in Bangkok. The best thing was that there wasn't a pasty camera-clicking tourist in sight – apart from me of course.

•

Time, I feel, to relax. I set off to visit Mina Sauna (Baños), meandering my way through the lesbians who were still demonstrating, past the square where the junkies get high, and past the decaying church, down a small side street that feels very Barcelona (cantinas with tables outside under the shade of lime trees).

Inside, the bathhouse was tiled, cool to the touch and quiet. I made my way upstairs, past a row of attendants smoking and watching on a blaring TV the ensuing war unfold, eyes transfixed with the intensity only football matches normally command. I asked for a cabin and an old Mexican with rotten teeth and a Zapata moustache assisted me. He leeringly winked at me as I struggled to understand the payment/key/deposit/another payment/towel system.

Having eventually secured my clothes in a locker I made my weary way to the shower room. The room was half full with as a motley selection of naked Mexicans as one could never wish to meet – they looked me up and down and then returned to chatting and bathing. I went into the steam room and suddenly discovered why the rest of the place was fairly quiet, because it was packed. Steam hissed intermittently, fogging the place, while men sat around gasping for breath or wiping their sweat-sedoak bodies down.

This, I was told, was not a gay sauna, strictly speaking, but looking around there seemed to be some cross-handed shuffles going on. I retreated, partly through the need to breathe, back to the showers, or should I say backs to the showers. It was much busier now and like a men's prison (or a Fassbinder's idea of a men's prison) – all soaping each other down, general rowdiness and camaraderie afoot as they twanged each other's half-stiff enchiladas.

I decided to get a massage, and returned to my cabin to negotiate with the attendant, miming that I required a massage. He nodded enthusiastically. He showed me to an adjacent room, pointed to a bed and indicated I lie down. Then I noticed he was beginning to take his clothes off.

'No, no, no,' I exclaimed. 'What you doing?' Seeing my concern he laughed, redressed and indicated he knew what I wanted, winking again, or maybe he had a twitch. Mexican twitch.

Several minutes later the door slammed open and a big strapping Aztec walked in and massaged me violently, nearly breaking every bone in my body – I wanted this to end as soon as it began. Now if this sounds pleasurable to you, remember it was a squalid room, with filthy towels, slimy slippery floor and war on Iraq booming outside on the TV. I know that it relieved my aches and pains, but pleasurable it was not. Then when he'd finished I tried to stand up, pummelled and kneaded like a bit of mouldy old masa, and he pointed at his groin, then towards my groin, smiled and

held out his hand, palm upwards (the universally acknowl-
edged gestures for money). I politely declined, tipped him,
made my excuses, dressed and left – I'd had enough 'shock
and awe' for one day.

•

I made a visit to the Zona Rosa, an upscale neighbourhood
filled with fancy restaurants and popular nightspots.

Mexico City has a very lively gay scene, with dozens of
bars and nightclubs to choose from, and Zona Rosa is where
a great many of them are situated. The downside is that they
are all much like every gay bar or club anywhere in the
world in what is a commercial village, though here there is a
higher proportion of lesbians than most. Zona Rosa is great
to walk around.

But be warned. As in many areas with heavy foot
traffic, you will encounter tourist rip-offs. It is advisable to
shop around before choosing a suitable bar or club. In the
evening, particularly on the weekends, the area becomes
crowded with people looking for a good time at neighbourhood discos and it is not uncommon for young men to hassle
people to go to the disco that they are promoting. I mean
really hassling. Don't be intimidated.

There is somewhere I discovered I'd rather be. Plaza
Garibaldi.

The Plaza Garibaldi is a favourite with the after-hours
crowd in Mexico City. The mariachi bands entertain those
who aren't too busy people-watching. Sleazy clubs, music
halls, burlesque houses, cheap eateries, and generally
extremely dodgy places surround the square. At night it
comes alive with sound and colour, and it is overwhelming.
There you can sip tequila, and feel truly like you are in
Mexico.

The only thing more Mexican than tequila is mariachi

and it's a shame to have one without the other. This square is the heart of mariachi, where hundreds of players and singers employ every trick known to vie for your attention.

The word mariachi refers to the musicians now commonly seen in restaurants or strolling the streets, dressed in silver-studded charro outfits with wide-brimmed hats, playing a variety of instruments which include violins, guitars, basses and trumpets. Their songs speak about machismo, love, betrayal, death, politics, revolutionary heroes and even animals (one particularly famous song is 'La Cucaracha' – the Cockroach).

Dressed in tight bottom-hugging pants, tiny black jackets and embroidered waistcoats and shirts, they serenade lovers, drinkers, the curious, anyone taking even a passing interest. For some loose change you can hire a mariachi, or even a whole band (you'll need more than change for that though) to follow you around; you can even take them home to serenade the wife. They stand along the strip touting for work, like surreal hookers with guitars, which in one respect they are, glorified gigolos – an exuberant carnival of vibrant colours and a cacophony of sound. They run up to cars and tout for business, guitar at the ready. It is mariachi mayhem and madness. They come in every age, shape and size, their outfits ranging from basic apparel through to rich-looking suits with abundant suede embroidery. I picked a small group and they serenaded me.

•

I finally did make it to the the Pyramid of the Sun.

Just outside Mexico City is Teotihuacán, 'the place where the gods were conceived', or 'the place where men became gods'. Aztec priests made pilgrimages to Teotihuacán, which was by then in ruins, remnants of a previous, still greater civilization about which almost nothing is known.

Teotihuacán is a remarkable site – a window looking onto an ancient civilization whose true identity no one knows for sure. There are three main areas: Ciudadela, the Pyramid of the Sun and the Pyramid of the Moon. They are all connected by the cheerily known 'Avenue of the Dead'.

I made the journey on our penultimate day, the sun beating down and my throat parched. As I approached the pyramid it began to loom larger and higher. Still some distance away, I could see figures, still tiny, climbing the staircase on some pilgrimage. Eventually I reached the base and began to climb, and climb. The steps are shallow and high, making footing precarious. On either side of the pyramid wall, which angles downwards, it is punctuated with jagged stones like dragon's teeth. I dared not look down or back, and reached the first plateau about a quarter way up, unable to venture near the edge for fear that my vertigo would kick in. Onwards to the next level, halfway, and by this time my breathing had become laboured, and I was feeling dizzy and nauseous. Octogenarians were sprinting past me by now but I didn't care. I hate fit old people, it's not right.

The blazing Mexican sun beat down, burning my head, but I could feel the spirit of the winged serpent god circling round me, and I pressed onwards and upwards. Well, by the time I got three-quarters up I was knackered. Now Mexican grandmothers, obese Americans and Japanese children were overtaking me, all made of sterner stuff.

I ventured on, but I have to be honest with you, I didn't make it to the summit. The final narrow climb, tourists easing up heel to nose, jostling for space and clinging on for dear life, for what? Actually in order to touch that sacred rock on the peak. But no, I thought, let them go, let them have their photo opportunity.

I walked along the ledge and sat on the corner of the

pyramid and took in the view of the entire site. This level of the pyramid provides the best view of the Avenue of the Dead, and somewhere in the back of my mind an orchestra began to swell. You can see the mountains in the far distance, the Pyramid of the Moon (only half the size of the Pyramid of the Sun), and a thin layer of gauze-like smog hanging over Mexico City. I sat there thinking about that kid I was in the school library, imagining myself on the top of this pyramid. I felt a sense of achievement and wonder. Maybe I didn't go to the top – I could have if I'd wanted, but I didn't. Sometimes it's best not to achieve all your goals, not to go all the way, leave something for later (the orchestra is building now). What I'm saying is happiness is knowing you could have but you saved something for another day.

And suddenly, yes, I felt like there was going to be another day. That was it, my midlife crisis and those middle-aged blues drifted out across the desert. There are new places to go and pleasure palaces to discover. For God's sake, it's not like I'm fifty – isn't that great, I'm still in my forties. Suddenly wrinkles, dirty bombs, those returned standing orders, the axis of evil, mass marketing, globalization, fast food, downloading my albums, cynical marketing, food additives – it all meant sod all: bring it on.

Bring them all on.

Bring on those prats who work in call centres that you have to deal with, bring on the apathetic nobodies who make my life hell when trying to get answers, bring on the terrible trains, bring on lying mobile tariffs, airlines that rip you off if you don't stay over a Saturday night, rude minicab drivers, those take a ticket and wait till your number's called queuing systems, bring on the two-faced balding bank managers, the rip-off DIY cowboys, those trumped-up tabloid exposés, celebrity halfwits, halfwit celebrities, pathetic political correctness, reality TV; bring on those black cabs with their lights on that don't stop, alcopops, cheese string, coca 'brain-rotting artificially sweetened chemical kiddie' cola, bring on extended warranties 'cos manufacturers can't guarantee the crap they sell you after six months; bring on lying insurance companies, take-forever teletext pages, junk mail, pop-ups, Geri, Robbie, ex-soap stars (stars huh?), karaoke, celebrity gossip, hype, bring on British Telecom's hidden charges, contracts, sequels, hymns, breakfast DJs, marijuana T-shirts, the furniture in furnished accommodation (the orchestra is reaching a crescendo) and know-it-all fucking people – so bring them all on, I don't care any more.

I'm going to live. Live life.

LIVE. (Camera pans away from me sitting on the edge of the Pyramid of the Sun until I'm a small dot in the far far distance, and then the pyramid itself is a small dot.)

Just me, my epiphany, a thousand tourists and an ancient monument. Just dots. Dots that are beginning to join.

•

The next day it was time to leave Mexico City for Moscow. I was feeling rejuvenated, feeling good, our soldiers were making sizeable advances in Iraq, and my mood is one of optimism from my epiphany on the pyramid.

But I'm not a teenager any more, and once again, to quote Burt Bacharach, 'There's always something there to remind me.'

I bent down to pick up my overweight suitcase (bulging from free toiletries) when I felt my back snap. My knees gave way and I lay on the floor in agony having slipped a disc. Calling for help, my companions came to my rescue with painkillers and a wheelchair – it must have been the pyramid trek, or that overenthusiastic masseur, or someone had put a curse on me at the voodoo market – whatever it was I was in agony.

Sitting in my wheelchair, being taken to the aircraft, I felt the effects of the painkillers kick in. I must make a note to hoodwink my doctor out of some of them – Vicodan and pethadin – terrific. Not for daily use of course but to hoard up for when the bomb or bombshell finally goes off – to paraphrase: 'hoarding up the drugs for the long winter of my death'.

Epilogue – London, August 2003

'The greatest thing you'll ever learn
Is just to love and be loved in return'
– 'Nature Boy', Eden Ahbez

•

Back home in south London I am sitting in one of my favourite restaurants, Champor Champor, with my old school friends, Stuart and Tim. We chat about the final part of this book and what I should write, and Tim begs me not to title this chapter 'There's No Place Like Home' – you know, as in Toto, Kansas and ruby slippers. I'm ashamed to say it had crossed my mind but it takes someone from Southport to stop someone from Southport being ... well, so Southport. It seems that I'll always be slightly uncool, however worldly I may claim to be.

The three of us sit in this exotic little hideaway in Bermondsey, sampling the jellyfish in coconut sauce, and discussing with the owner Charles the secret of his fabulous smoked-banana ice cream. He tells us the bananas are sourced from a tiny rural village in Malaysia where they are smoked over a local timber, and then flown (still warm I imagine) to Britain, just so this restaurant can conjure up the house speciality. I am sure he wouldn't mind me mentioning this because if it were my smoked-banana ice cream in my own restaurant (if I had one) then I would be telling everybody. All the time. How small the world suddenly seems to me that one day a banana is smouldering over some hot ash in a tropical rainforest in the back and beyond of Malaysia, and the next day it's slipping down my gullet somewhere in south London. Now that must mean something, but quite what I haven't got a clue.

Now we're middle-aged men reminiscing about the thirty years or more since, as teenagers, we had our 'listening to records' afternoons, miming to Bowie or Roxy or raving over the merits of the latest Eno and Nico collaboration, while gorging ourselves on Tim's mother's home-made cream cakes; and remembering how full of youth, for want of a better word, we were.

Stuart is now a restaurant critic and food author, and Tim sells under-the-counter porn videos in a Soho sex shop; me, well, I've been known to sing a song or two. So in the end we all deal in pleasure – a fine meal, a great song, and a good wank.

Catching up with old friends can be a pleasurable part of revisiting the past and, as I found out, a necessary one. Answers to questions, bridges to rebuild, ghosts to lay to rest, that sort of thing. It reminds us of who we are, where we came from and the roads we have travelled. Time heals, scars fade, and sitting with Tim and Stuart we forget the times we all fell out, like when I got in with a bad crowd at school and tried to be someone I wasn't, allying myself with the enemy in some naive attempt to fit in, avoid confrontation and gain acceptance. How many years did I continue to do that for? It took a long hard road, many years of drug addiction, breakdowns and psychotic episodes to get even an inkling that I was deluding myself.

Not so long ago I had one of the best nights in years visiting old friends: a school reunion with some of my classmates of Aireborough Grammar '71. It took place in a country pub outside Nottingham. As I waited for my taxi at the local hotel to take me to the rendezvous, so many thoughts and feelings went through my head – nervous excitement through to sheer panic, feelings that I couldn't rationalize. But curiosity spurred me on. Faces I hadn't seen in over thirty years. I felt in many ways at a disadvantage because of course they knew what I looked like, what I'd done, how I had aged, but for me it was a mystery tour.

And walking into the pub, there they all were, just as I had left them but of course not the same, yet somehow still quite familiar. It was a chance for me to say how they had, each in their own way, made school more bearable for me, a chance to fill in the gaps about what was going on in our lives; a chance for confessions, revelations, you know the sort of thing.

The entertainment was provided by Chris Halliday (whom I mentioned in *Tainted Life*), now a teacher but also a singer. It was nice to have someone sing to me for a change. Meeting up with these old friends after so many years was an odd experience – eyeing each other up, looking for recognizable traits, seeing the changes, the altered appearance, the lines or three, the extra weight, greying hairs, life's battle scars. But strangely, after a while, we all change back into how we were and revert to classmates.

I left the reunion feeling elated, on a high, something of a line drawn under the past. It was the perfect group therapy meeting.

As recovering addicts go, I know that I am not the best example. I know that Dr Lefever (the head of the Promis treatment centre who oversaw my recovery from addiction) would reprimand me for not attending NA meetings with the regularity he recommended. But I make things work for me through my work, my recording and performing. I still occasionally obsess about pills and drugs, but less and less, sometimes forgetting them altogether for long periods: and most importantly throughout I never pick up. Do anything it takes but never use.

And ecstasy and cocaine? I always find myself being asked about them during interviews, probably because they make the best tabloid rock and roll stories. Somehow prescription drugs don't seem as glamorous by half.

•

Revisiting my past in music was to me a success, by which I mean re-forming Soft Cell. Getting older means getting realistic, and success is downsized like everything else. We made a great album, got positive reviews, raised profiles, regenerated back catalogue, staged exciting shows, made fans happy (maybe happy isn't the right word), got a Top 40 single, made a bit of money and enjoyed a degree of success.

So it went a little pear-shaped at the end when we ran out of our allotted time, but weighing up the positives against the negatives it all evened out in the end.

If we hadn't re-formed Soft Cell then we'd always have wondered, what if? Indeed. And besides, no one died.

Would I do it again? Hell, you know that I've learned to say 'never say never'. Again.

Of course there were the doom mongers who condemned what I did even before they had heard it. While I used to take my work far too seriously, now others seem to do that for me.

I've discovered that the most important thing in life is having a life.

Having a life has become a priority.

Learning to enjoy it and celebrate it.

The year 2004 marks my twenty-five years in the music business, and whichever way you look at it that's not bad going – I've still got a public profile, still making records, doing concerts, making a living. And you know what, people tell me I was a major musical influence, and they even tell me I'm still a star, and I think they might be right because people still (amazingly I know) give into my demands. Most importantly I can still get a good table at the Ivy, and that is, when all is said and done, the measure of true success.

Sitting back in my downsized bedroom in my downsized apartment, looking out across the London skyline I realize at last that I have been lucky. I've learned about irony, which nowadays has seen me through. Irony is just about being the first in there to laugh at yourself, before everyone else does, even if it means crying in private. Actually irony is so many things to me that I thought I'd share a few with you, that someone shared with me.

> It's a death row pardon two minutes too late.
> It's a free ride when you've already paid.
> It's good advice you didn't take.
> A no smoking sign on your cigarette break.
> *It's like watching Gene Pitney on TV when you're*
>   *young*
> *And years later duet on his most famous song*
>   *(with him, no less)*
> *And improbably watch it hit number one.*

I suppose what I'm talking about is that irony is like being on stage with Frank Sinatra, me and Frank, imagine that, the pinnacle of my career and Frank calls me by name, but the wrong name.

•

Flicking back and forth on the TV it seems we're really crawling around in the cathode sewer, back where I was at before I made this journey. An immediate surf through the channels reveals a variety of dubious programming: a docu-soap about strippers, a documentary about cracked-up celebrities, fifty ways to satisfy your man (principally aimed at women, I guess, though I learned something new, even at my age) 'humming': during the act of popping one or more testicles in your mouth (one seems enough) and humming, thus creating a vibrating effect, enhancing stimulation. So many fascinating facts – that was number 18 in the countdown.

I flick over.

A show about Jordan (the model, not the country) as she prowls a succession of nightclubs eeking out C-list celebrities to devour in full tabloid splendour.

Another channel is showing a documentary about the porn king Seymour Butts and his family porn film empire. Seymour is talking us through the filming of his new movies *Squirters 2* and *Ass-Gasm*, and I'm not even on cable yet.

My point is that it's all out there if you want it, and appearing in your living room as soon as you like.

There is a theme here. Just trash. And what can you do, you can't fight it, you can't lose sleep over it, just ignore it or give in. I accept now there is no point despairing that there are not enough blurry subtitled films on TV or art programmes, this is where we are. Where once I despaired now I embrace our trash culture.

•

I give in.

I throw off this curse of midlife crisis, and say I denounce it.

I'm beat. Middle age doesn't frighten me any more.

There, I'm over that. My journey to the places of my past, my early inspirations, choices and paths I made has filled me with hope. I suppose I wanted to take a walk on the wild side, if only to discover what is not me. I used to live the part but now more often than not I'm playing it.

What I want now in my life is beauty – it inspires me, uplifts me, it fills me with a sense of positivity, wonderment and, as Dostoevsky said, 'Beauty will save the world.' Thinking about it maybe he meant, 'The beauty that will save the world is the love that shares the pain.'

•

Life, I have discovered, is like addiction – the only way to get through it is to surrender. The more you struggle, the more entwined you become, and only submission can set you free, set you on the road to serenity. My addiction was simply clinging to something in desperation even though it was harmful to me – it was my search for feelings that had become anaesthetized long ago. But I have to say addiction mixes pleasure with guilt, and is a combination that can seduce you by being more alluring than pleasure alone. That's the trap you get entangled in: not attaining so much pleasure that you can override the feelings of guilt, and simultaneously not suffering so much that you can choose to end the pleasure.

Accept the inevitable, that all that really matters are fleeting moments of real pleasure that collectively will add up to a life.

All those travels and explorations made me realize that the one place I hadn't had the courage to visit was myself, not honestly and certainly not inwardly. I assumed that as long as I kept moving I could catch something of meaning, but at some point I stopped and admired the view, and in doing so it dawned on me that happiness was in the simple moments when I never imagined being unhappy. Moments of utter clarity.

Standing alone on Southport beach in winter, Christmases, a feeling of being home. Or standing in New York in Times Square and letting it engulf you, sitting in Time Cafe with old friends and a familiar menu, or Scott DJ'ing trashy tunes at the Cock Club whilst lonely go-go dancers pour disdain on adoring punters.

These are the jewels, the treasures.

In Paris it is simply walking around Pigalle as songs drift from smoky bars, sitting on the sidewalk sipping a drink, or watching the girls in spangly outfits on their swings at the Crazy Horse.

Amsterdam is breakfast by the canal, just as the city wakes (always a late sleeper), and watching the day yawn and stretch, the light dance on the green water of the canals, or the smell of musky leather in the bars.

Priceless snapshots.

Barcelona is sitting in Plaza Real lunching on grilled sardines, tomato bread and paella.

LA is driving in an open-topped car down a boulevard to nowhere, silhouetted palms against the Hollywood sign, a glorious smog-infused blood-orange sunset.

In Las Vegas it was that moment hanging weightless in mid-air after being catapulted to the top of Stratosphere, 1,200 feet above the Strip, looking out across the whole of the city and the tar blackness of the desert.

Rome is just Rome, breathtaking, walking around and trying to comprehend that so much beauty is in the world, conceived by men; the sound of laughter, the whir of scooters, teenagers with great skin, in love.

And Mexico, the tranquillity of sitting in Frida Kahlo's shaded garden, and sipping tea by Garibaldi Square, lost in the surreality of it.

Then of course so many moments in Russia, but one in particular stands out: an autumn evening standing on a bridge at the bottom of Red Square, looking out over the

Kremlin, the spires and domes of reflected gold, a skein of cranes flying overhead, and the first flakes of snow beginning to drift earthward. Looking down along the sweeping curve of the River Neva to see outlined in the distance one of Stalin's gothic buildings. This was just a moment caught in time, a photo of a memory.

It makes me think of an old Russian saying:

Don't keep looking backwards, you might not see the stairs.

Moments.

Indulge in the past but don't live in it. It's strange how many of my moments, those recollections that I've put together (that have enabled me to cast off the doubts of middle age), are no more than walks or of stillness. All these years and all this time I'd been running away from myself, only to discover of course that wherever I went, there I was. But I've since discovered that I'm actually worth more than I gave myself credit for, and I've actually come to like myself, and I can't believe it's taken me so many years and so many miles to find that out.

•

I have this dream that keeps coming back to me.

I am on stage in this enormous theatre having just performed, taking a bow. But I am also in the audience watching myself up on the stage. And though I recognize myself on the stage I feel completely detached from him.

The curtain slowly closes, heavy red velvet drapes with a gold fringe. A spotlight hits the centre of the stage, and then forms a perfect circle where the curtains meet.

The audience start applauding wildly. Gradually they rise from their seats in a standing ovation, thunderous stamping and clapping resonating around the auditorium.

A gloved hand appears around the curtain (let them know you're coming) and the applause builds into a cheering crescendo.

Bravo. Bravo.

The camera pans in for a close-up of hand clutching a bejewelled microphone. A frail figure shuffles precariously through the curtains into the spotlight, infirm and unsteady. His familiar face appears younger than his gait would suggest, taut, translucent, perspiring, mascara running a little down the thick white pan stick. Only the wrinkle folds of his neck betray his age.

The audience bay and cheer.

Encores.

Epilogues and encores.

It's never easy to end anything, not when there's a drop of adulation still to be wrung out.

Camera pans back. Conductor raises his baton, momentarily holds the gesture in mid air, sweeps his arm downwards and the music begins. Audience fall instantly silent. Sitting. Respectfully still.

Clearing his throat I begin to sing.

> I'm just a gigolo
> And everywhere I go
> People know the part I'm playing

Camera pans slowly upwards to reveal the whole stage, the blood-red backcloth. An enormous illuminated sign reads '50 Year Anniversary Concert', a single spot, the lone figure emoting, a decrepit hand outstretched breaching the invisible wall between artist and audience, reaching out, for acceptance, for acknowledgement, adoration, for . . . love.

The camera pans upwards, framing the stage below, up past the lights, through the flies, the rigging, sweeping around cables and wires, across walkways, upwards into the dusty roof of the theatre where two elderly stagehands sit drinking tea from flasks and eating egg sandwiches, their feet dangling over the edge of the walkway. They lean over to watch the tiny figure hundreds of feet below, the singing drifting upwards.

> . . . what will they say about me?
> When the end comes I know
> They'll say just a gigolo

> and . . .

> life . . .

> goes on . . .

> without me.